American History
in No Time

R. Russell

American History in No Time

A Quick & Easy Read for the Basics

Randolph G. Russell

Life At

ISBN-13: 978-0-9679214-2-6

CONTENTS

INTRODUCTION

The history of America is an amazing story but all too unfamiliar. *American History in No Time* is a quick and easy way to learn the basics. In just a few hours you will know the key events, people, places, and principles from pre-Columbian times to the present. This overview concentrates on that part of North America that became the United States.

On the next page you will find a timeline of the last 500 years. Six key events are already plotted. As you can see, the Civil War is closer to us in time than the beginning of Jamestown was to the Founders of the United States. A map showing the territorial expansion of the U.S. and a world map are also provided. As you progress through the book, refer back to the timeline and the maps to enhance your perspective.

Learning about the past is an enriching experience. Wherever you live or wherever you go in this country, people have lived there or passed that way for centuries or even millennia. That realization fosters curiosity about the way things used to be and what the people were like.

One of the purposes of this book is to instill a sense of history and a desire to know more. Then, perhaps, while vacationing at Disney World in Orlando, you will also want to visit St. Augustine, an early Spanish colonial outpost and the oldest European settlement in the continental United States, just two hours away. After visiting the Gateway Arch in St. Louis, you will want to head 10 miles east to Cahokia and climb to the top of Monks Mound, an ancient Native American earthen structure with a larger footprint than the Great Pyramid of Giza in Egypt. If you go to the French Quarter in New Orleans for Mardi Gras you will stop at the corner of St. Louis and Chartres streets, where slaves were auctioned before the Civil War. If you travel to Las Vegas you might plan a side trip to an old mining town nearby called Rhyolite, now a ghost town. And while in New York City, after taking in a show at Madison Square Garden or on Broadway, you will want to go to Wall Street, the financial center of the country, and stand next to the statue of George Washington, on the spot where he took the oath of office in 1789 as the first president of the United States.

The past is all around us, and it provides an unlimited supply of fascinating stories. Looking back gives us a better perspective of our place in the world, helps us recognize how valuable our time is, makes us appreciate the struggles and successes of those who preceded us, and encourages us to make our own contributions to the country.

Now, the basics.

Timeline

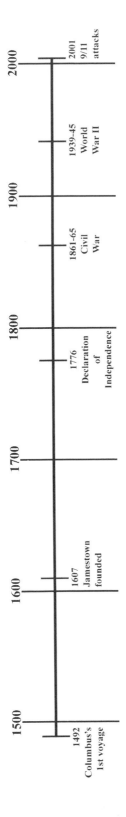

1500

1492
Columbus's
1st voyage

1600

1607
Jamestown
founded

1700

1776
Declaration
of
Independence

1800

1861-65
Civil
War

1900

1939-45
World
War II

2000

2001
9/11
attacks

Territorial Acquisitions

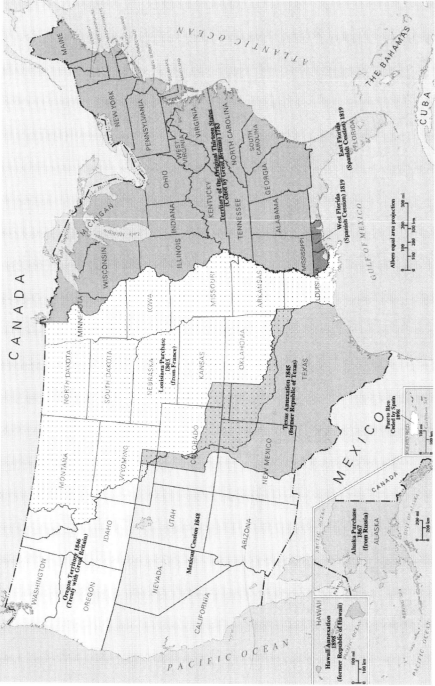

U.S. Geological Survey

World Map

ANCIENT AMERICA

Archaeologists do not know how the Western Hemisphere was first populated, but most believe that Asian hunter-gatherers migrated through Alaska. The principal weapon of the earliest inhabitants was the spear.*

American civilization entered a new stage of development with the adoption of agriculture. It began in the middle or "meso" region of the hemisphere, from Central Mexico to Nicaragua. Three crops rose to prominence as staples: the "Three Sisters" or agricultural trinity of corn (maize), beans, and squash. Other native foods, including pumpkins, potatoes, avocados, pineapples, tomatoes, peanuts, vanilla, and cocoa, were also cultivated in the hemisphere. Early peoples tilled the land without the aid of plows or draft animals.†

Agriculture provided more predictable, accessible, and plentiful food resources and made settlement possible in more areas. Groups that farmed continued to hunt and gather, however, to obtain medicinal plants and supplement their food supply.

Farming started to take hold in what is now the United States around 2000 B.C. It was conducive to permanent settlement but not a prerequisite. In areas where wild food resources were abundant, hunter-gatherer communities were able to thrive.

Ancient Americans did not live isolated from one another. They entered into alliances for warfare and crossed geographic, linguistic, cultural, and tribal boundaries to trade. Copper from the Great Lakes, mica from the Carolinas, turquoise from Arizona, obsidian from the Rocky Mountains, and shells from the coasts have been unearthed in graves and other archaeological sites hundreds and even thousands of miles away. Ideas, technologies, religious practices, language, and labor were also exchanged, and there was intermarrying between groups.

None of the indigenous people north of Mexico developed a written language, but linguists have identified hundreds of spoken tongues. Native Americans used sign language to bridge communication barriers. Petroglyphs (images carved into rocks) and pictographs (painted images) were other forms of communication as well as artistic expressions.

---

* *The bow and arrow would not be in use throughout the present-day United States until 700 A.D.*

† *Horses, cows, oxen, and plows were all brought to the Americas from the Eastern Hemisphere. Prior to European contact, the indigenous people of North America domesticated turkeys and dogs. Some dogs pulled sleds and served as pack animals.*

INDIGENOUS CULTURES

Native Americans are not a single, homogeneous people. When Europeans arrived in the present-day United States, there were hundreds of tribes within diverse cultures broadly defined by geographic region: the Pacific Coast, the Plateau, the Great Basin, the Southwest, the Great Plains, and the Eastern Woodlands. Their customs, beliefs, survival strategies, political systems, and economies had evolved over millennia.

The abundant natural resources of the Pacific Coast supported one of the densest indigenous populations. The diversity of the environment spawned cultural diversity and numerous languages.

Few Pacific Coast tribes farmed, even after European contact. They harvested marine life, hunted large and small game in the forests, and gathered seeds, nuts, roots, and berries. Meat and seafood were preserved for long periods through drying and smoking. Salmon were a major food source for people in the Pacific Northwest, including the Chinook, Salish, and Makah tribes, who also hunted seals and took whales using large ocean-going dugout canoes.

Acorns, which had to be leached to be edible, were the staple of the Chumash, Ohlone, Pomo, and other California tribes. Their tightly woven baskets could hold water and were used for cooking. Stones heated over a fire were placed in the water along with the food. Constantly stirring the hot stones kept the inside of the basket from being scorched while the food cooked.

Round, single-family thatched dwellings were typical in California. Tribes in the Pacific Northwest lived in cedar plank lodges, usually built to house an extended family. In Washington and in areas farther north, the people carved and painted the structural beams of their houses with elaborate images depicting animals, supernatural beings, family legends, and honored ancestors. The practice was carried over to large free-standing cedar trunks, or totem poles, erected in front of dwellings and at burial sites. Totem poles also served as status symbols.

Another demonstration of social status in the Pacific Northwest was the potlatch. These lavish celebrations marking important family events, such as births and marriages, were also occasions to display and distribute one's wealth to invited guests. The giving of extravagant gifts enhanced the host family's prestige and obligated recipients of the largesse to reciprocate with potlatches of their own. At some gatherings, possessions were destroyed as an ostentatious show of affluence.

The Plateau region in Idaho, western Montana, and the eastern parts of Washington and Oregon was home to semi-nomadic tribes: the Nez Perce, the Yakama, the Palouse, and others. They built pit houses and grass or wood huts for shelter. Tule mats were used for flooring and additional exterior coverings.

Tribes hunted bear, deer, and elk and used antlers to dig up wild roots and bulbs, especially camas. They also exploited the return of spawning salmon and trout to inland waterways. A variety of fishing gear was used, including nets, weirs, bone hooks, and plant poisons to stun the fish for easy capture.

Among some Plateau tribes, funerals lasted for days, and the dwelling and other possessions of the deceased were burned.

A different native culture developed in the Great Basin. This predominantly desert environment lying between the Sierra Nevada mountain range and the Rocky Mountains comprises most of Nevada and Utah and lesser portions of the surrounding states. Rainfall and other water resources vary widely.

The region's Ute, Washoe, Shoshone, and Paiute tribes were mobile hunter-gatherers. Their food came primarily from plants, with piñon nuts being the staple. Rabbits, antelope, and bighorn sheep provided meat and skins. Waterfowl were taken with the aid of snares and well-crafted floatable duck decoys. The most common Native American dwelling in the Great Basin was a brush hut stabilized with rocks piled around the outer base.

In the 1500s Spanish conquistadors pushed northward from Mexico into the American Southwest. In present-day New Mexico, Arizona, and parts of neighboring states, they found the inhabitants living in numerous towns and villages. Spaniards called the natives "Pueblos," the Spanish word for towns. The Hopi and the Zuni were the principal tribes in the region. The Anasazi, Mogollon, and Hohokam were predecessor cultures.

From ancient times, Pueblos relied mainly on agriculture for their subsistence. Using hillside terracing, dams, rainwater collection, and irrigation, they made the most of the available water and were able to produce two crop yields per year on arid land. Those living near rivers dug irrigation canals using only stone and wood tools. Some canals were up to 25 feet wide and 10 feet deep; the longest stretched for 16 miles. Canal builders carefully analyzed the topography before choosing a route, and the slope and width of canals were precisely engineered to produce a steady flow.

Even though the wheel was not used for transportation in the Western Hemisphere prior to European contact, Pueblo Indians constructed hundreds of miles of remarkably straight roads as wide as 30 feet in places. Roads fostered interaction and trade between the towns. Pueblos also traded their dyed cotton fabrics, turquoise jewelry, decorated baskets and pottery, and agricultural goods with indigenous groups outside the region, from as far away as Central Mexico and the Pacific Coast.

The most distinctive Pueblo structures were contiguous, multi-story, apartment-like buildings made of stone or adobe and situated high atop mesas, down on canyon floors, or in large caves in the walls of cliffs. Some of the structures contained hundreds of rooms.

Kivas were prominent features in the towns. These enclosed chambers, usually circular and built below ground, were used for religious and social gatherings.

Spanish colonization of the American West began in Pueblo territory in 1598 and included the building of Catholic missions to spread Christianity. To maintain their advantage in mobility, Spaniards kept horses out of the hands of the indigenous people, who traveled and hunted on foot.

Hoping to rid themselves of foreign domination, return to their traditional ways, and avenge Spanish abuses, Pueblo Indians in 1680 mounted a carefully planned attack organized by Popé, a native religious leader. They killed 400 Spanish colonists along with 21 friars. A thousand survivors of the Pueblo Revolt fled south to El Paso, leaving their livestock behind. Pueblos used the horses to barter with tribes from outside the region, and the animal spread across the continent and became an integral part of the broader Native American culture.

Navajo Indians, enemies of the Pueblos, entered the Southwest a century or two before the Spaniards and eventually became the largest tribe. Originally a nomadic people, Navajos adopted agriculture and sheepherding and became expert weavers. They dwelled in earthen lodges called hogans but did not establish villages, preferring instead to live in individual families or family clusters apart from others.

The Great Plains, an expanse of prairie with flat grasslands, few forests, and little rainfall, lie between the Rocky Mountains and the Mississippi River. Millions of bison (or buffalo) roamed the region. Most tribes on the Great Plains, including the Blackfoot, Sioux, Arapaho, Cheyenne, Apache, and Comanche, followed migrations of the gigantic herds. Flesh from the large animal provided food. Its hide was used for clothing, shelter, blankets, and rope. Its bones and horns were fashioned into weapons, tools, and ornaments. The bladder was used as a water container, and thread was made from the sinews. Dried bison dung provided fuel for fires.

Nomadic Plains Indians lived in teepees: portable, cone-shaped structures framed with wooden poles and covered with tanned buffalo hides. Sedentary Plains tribes, who hunted buffalo only seasonally, lived in grass or earthen shelters.

In the woodlands east of the Mississippi River, permanent settlements began to appear before the adoption of agriculture. The indigenous people subsisted on deer, turkey, fish, waterfowl, and wild plants, in particular, hickory nuts and acorns.

A trade network operated within the region and as far west as the Rocky Mountains. The birchbark canoe, an ingenious invention so light it could be carried by one person, facilitated travel over inland waterways.

Mounds were a peculiar feature of early Eastern Woodlands cultures. Some of the earthen structures formed geometric shapes and patterns or were made to depict animals (effigy mounds). Others served as burial sites or flat-topped platforms for temples and dwellings of the elite. More than a thousand earthworks have been identified, built as early as 3500 B.C. during the archaic period, later by the Adena and Hopewell cultures, and finally by the Mississippian culture, which lasted to around 1500 A.D. Artifacts uncovered at these sites – tools, jewelry, stonework, shell-tempered pottery, and hammered metalwork – display a high degree of artistry and technical skill.

One of the most impressive archaic sites is at Poverty Point in northeastern Louisiana. The earthworks there consist of six concentric semi-circles that curve around a central plaza. The rings, which some researchers believe originally formed a complete circle, are 140 to 200 feet apart, range in width from 40 to 90 feet, and stand 4 to 6 feet high. The outer ring is nearly a mile in diameter. The purpose of the structure is unknown.

The largest single mound yet discovered, Monks Mound, was built at Cahokia, a major urban center of the Mississippian culture. The city was located 10 miles east of present-day St. Louis, Missouri, a fertile area near the confluence of the Mississippi and Missouri Rivers. At its peak, Cahokia had a population of between 10,000 and 20,000. Flint tools were manufactured there.

The construction of Monks Mound began circa 900 A.D. and continued for 200 years. The tiered pyramid contains 22 million cubic feet of dirt, rises in four terraces to a height of 100 feet, and has a base area of 16 acres, a larger footprint than the Pyramid of the Sun in Mexico or the Great Pyramid of Giza in Egypt.

Cahokians erected 120 smaller mounds within a five-square-mile area.

Less than a mile from Monks Mound lies a site that has been called "America's Woodhenge." Cahokians placed cedar posts vertically in the ground to form a circle hundreds of feet in diameter. A single post was erected in the center. From that vantage point, three of the outer posts aligned with the solstices and equinoxes.

By the time French explorers came upon Cahokia in the 1600s, the city had been abandoned, its inhabitants had dispersed to smaller settlements, and the long tradition of mound building was coming to an end.

Northern tribes in the Eastern Woodlands included the Algonquin, Wampanoag, Shawnee, Powhatan, and Iroquois.

The Iroquois held women in high regard and traced kinship through the maternal line. When a couple married, they lived in the home of the wife's family. The penalty for killing a woman was twice that for killing a man. Iroquois women could dictate political actions such as whether or not to wage war. The clan mother nominated the male chief, who represented them at tribal councils. She could also depose him.

The traditional Iroquois dwelling was the longhouse, a large rectangular structure that sheltered an extended family. The wood frame, typically 20 feet wide, 20 feet high, and more than 100 feet long, was covered with sheets of bark. Smoke from indoor fires escaped through holes built into arched or gabled roofs.

The wigwam was another common dwelling among northern woodlands tribes. Branches or felled saplings were fixed in the ground, then bent over and lashed together to form a dome-shaped frame, which was covered with bark, hides, or thatching.

Among southern tribes – the Cherokee, Choctaw, Chickasaw, and Creek – wattle and daub dwellings were prevalent. Branches, vines, or strips of wood were woven together to form a lattice frame (wattle) that was coated with a mud plaster (daub). Roofs were thatched or shingled with bark.

Estimates of the size of pre-Columbian populations in North and South America vary widely. The population north of Mexico, thought to have been between one and 15 million, was small relative to the entire population of the hemisphere, believed to have been between eight and 100 million. Whatever the correct figures are, it is generally accepted that the population decreased dramatically following European contact.

Over the centuries, Europeans had built up a natural resistance to smallpox, measles, and other diseases common in the Eastern Hemisphere. Native Americans had no such immunity. When they were exposed, the results were devastating. Millions died. The indigenous population of the Western Hemisphere is estimated to have declined by as much as 90 percent in the first hundred years after Europeans arrived.

3
COLUMBUS

In the 1400s silk, cotton, spices, and other goods from South and East Asia (the Indies) were sought after in Europe, but transporting them was slow, costly, and dangerous. Trade routes between the two continents were entirely over land or a combination of land and sea. An all-sea route would have significant advantages. Sailing ships could travel day and night and haul heavy loads with relative ease compared with pack animals and wagons. Loading and unloading would be necessary only at the beginning and end of a journey, and middlemen along the existing routes could be bypassed and their fees avoided.

While other European explorers pursued an eastward sea route to the Indies around the southern tip of Africa, Christopher Columbus, an Italian, believed sailing west across the Atlantic Ocean would be more direct. He tried for years to gain support for such a voyage until King Ferdinand and Queen Isabella of Spain agreed to sponsor him.

The 40-year-old Columbus set sail from Spain in August of 1492 with a crew of 88 men on three ships: the *Niña*, the *Pinta*, and the flagship, the *Santa Maria*. Following a month-long stopover in the Canary Islands, just off the northwest coast of Africa, the expedition headed out over the Atlantic. In the early morning hours of October 12, after five weeks at sea, they sighted a small island and went ashore later that day.

Believing he had reached the Indies and proven his theory, Columbus called the inhabitants "Indians." But he was not in Asia. The ships had landed in the Bahamas, an island chain that was part of the North American continent. The shores of a vast mainland were just 400 miles farther west. A second continent lay 800 miles to the south. Both continents were unknown to Europeans of the day.

Columbus explored Cuba and other islands in the Caribbean, claimed the lands for Spain, and planted a colony on the island of Hispaniola* before sailing back to Europe. His return after the seven-month expedition was met with much fanfare. The voyage marked the beginning of the Columbian Exchange: the widespread transfer of animals, plants, human populations, ideas, and diseases between the two hemispheres.

Over the next 11 years, Columbus made three more voyages for Spain, exploring South America and other parts of North America but never setting foot on the mainland of the present-day United States. Notwithstanding his discoveries, what Europeans called a New World, Columbus died in relative obscurity. Neither continent bears his name.

Amerigo Vespucci was a member of at least two expeditions to the Western Hemisphere after 1492, none of which he commanded. Nevertheless, Vespucci's writings led some to believe that he was the discoverer. Consequently, the Americas were named after this minor explorer.

Hispaniola is currently divided between the countries of Haiti and the Dominican Republic.

4
THE LOST COLONY

Following Spain's lead, other European countries sponsored voyages to the Western Hemisphere and laid claim to territory. An English expedition in 1497 led by another Italian explorer, John Cabot, was the basis for England's territorial claims in North America, but those claims were not pursued for almost a century.

Colonization of the Americas helped Spain become the dominant power in the Western world. English privateers challenged that position by seizing Spanish merchant ships hauling gold, silver, and other commodities from the New World. Sir Walter Raleigh, one of the English mariners or "sea dogs" carrying out the raids, convinced Queen Elizabeth I that a colony in America would be a valuable base of operations and help England compete economically.

In 1587 the English planted a colony on Roanoke, an island midway up the Atlantic coast of North America. They called the region Virginia, in honor of their Virgin Queen, Elizabeth.

When a relief ship arrived from England three years later, the Roanoke settlement was deserted. What happened to the Lost Colony remains a mystery. Among the missing 115 settlers was Virginia Dare, the first English child born in America.

As a result of the failure, Queen Elizabeth lost interest in colonization across the Atlantic. England's next attempt would come during the reign of her successor.

JAMESTOWN

King James I supported colonizing America to thwart Spanish and French expansion, exploit a new source of raw materials, reduce overpopulation and unemployment in England, and spread Protestant Christianity. He granted a company the right to establish a new English colony in Virginia.

Investors in the London Company expected to profit from the export of precious metals, forestry products, and agricultural goods, and they hoped colonists would find the Northwest Passage, a continuous water route believed to cut through North America to the Pacific Ocean. Such a trade route to the Orient would give England a distinct economic advantage.

Three company ships with 104 colonists on board set sail from England in December of 1606. After a five-month voyage via the Canary Islands and the Caribbean, they arrived in the Chesapeake Bay a hundred miles north of Roanoke Island. Sailing up one of the rivers emptying into the bay in search of a place to plant the colony, they settled on a peninsula jutting out into the river some 40 miles inland. Water near the shoreline was deep enough for their large ships to be moored to trees on the bank, which made unloading and loading more convenient. The peninsula's distance from the bay minimized the chance of attack by Spanish or French warships.

The site was a poor choice overall, however. The surrounding land, low and marshy, was a breeding ground for disease, and fresh water was not readily available, particularly in the summer. The region was in the midst of a severe drought that began in 1606 and would last until 1612. As the water level of the river fell, salt water from the Chesapeake Bay moved farther upriver, making water drawn from the river and from shallow wells unsuitable for drinking. The contaminated water would soon sap the strength of the Englishmen and make them sick.

The settlers named the river and the colony after their king. Jamestown began in May of 1607 under a communal arrangement. The company claimed all rights to the land. Colonists were obligated to work for the company and for the welfare of the group in return for passage, support after their arrival, and a share of the profits.

After building a triangular fort and a few simple structures inside the one-acre enclosure, they wasted time and energy searching for gold, which did not exist in the area. Half of the colonists were gentlemen from upper-class families and were unaccustomed to the manual labor necessary for survival in a wilderness. They believed such work was beneath them.

The conditions were formidable, and provisions brought from England were insufficient. In the first four months, over half the colonists died, mostly from disease. The arrival of supplies and more settlers from England over the next two years (including the first women) helped temporarily, but the newcomers were just as ill-suited to the demands of the colony.

Maintaining adequate stores of food was a constant challenge, particularly in a drought. Company leaders in England failed to recognize the urgency of making Jamestown self-sufficient, and colonists relied too heavily on supply ships from England and trade with the Indians.

Although the company instructed the settlers to take "great care not to offend the naturals," the mere presence of foreigners was enough to spark conflict, especially as local Powhatan tribes realized the English intended to establish a permanent settlement. The Native Americans were fascinated with glass beads, mirrors, copper kettles, and other English goods and were willing to trade their surplus food to obtain them, but the colonists' persistent demands for provisions strained relations. Both sides carried out attacks and reprisals.

Captain John Smith assumed the leadership of Jamestown and imposed strict discipline, warning: "He that will not work shall not eat." Smith kept the colony in reasonably good condition until he was injured in a gunpowder accident and returned to England.

The winter after Smith's departure was called "the starving time." Indians laid siege to Jamestown, making it dangerous to venture outside the fort to obtain food. Colonists ate snakes, rats, horsehides, and shoe leather in a struggle to survive. Some resorted to cannibalizing the dead. When supply ships arrived in 1610, only 60 feeble colonists were still alive; six months earlier the population had been 350. Given this seemingly hopeless situation, the commander of the ships thought it best to load up all the colonists and return to England.

Halfway down the James River, the departing colonists met a small boat carrying an advance party of new arrivals from England. They brought word that three large ships were sailing up the river with abundant provisions, 150 settlers, and a newly appointed leader. The Jamestown survivors were told to turn back.

The situation slowly improved. Allocating land to the colonists for their personal use had a dramatic effect. Settlers worked harder on their own land than they did on land belonging to the company. With the end of the drought, food shortages became a thing of the past.

In 1614 colonist John Rolfe married Pocahontas, the daughter of the principal tribal chief in the area, after she converted to Christianity. Their marriage brought a temporary peace between the two peoples.

Tobacco, native to the Americas, played a key role in establishing the colony. The leaf smoked by the Powhatans was bitter. Colonists experimented with a mild and fragrant variety of the plant brought up from the Caribbean. It grew well in Virginia, and high demand in England made tobacco Jamestown's main export. Expanding tobacco plantations further encroached on Indian territories, though, which increased tensions.

In 1619 representative government was introduced when delegates from Jamestown and nearby settlements met to make laws for the entire Virginia colony. Their assembly, the House of Burgesses, was the first elected legislative body in the Western Hemisphere.*

It took time for Jamestown to become secure, and the death toll remained high for years, but the town survived and took its place in history as the first permanent English settlement in the New World.

As for Pocahontas – in 1616 she and John Rolfe and their infant son sailed to England, where she was a celebrated visitor. The following year, just as the family was setting out on the return voyage to America, Pocahontas became seriously ill and died. Only 22 years old, she was buried in England.

* *Jamestown remained the capital of the Virginia colony for 80 years. In 1699 the colonial government moved six miles away to a new capital, Williamsburg.*

6
NEW ENGLAND

The Protestant Reformation in England had begun in the 1530s with King Henry VIII's rejection of papal authority and the founding of the Church of England, or Anglican Church. Those seeking further reforms faced opposition. The hardships they suffered for their beliefs caused them to look to America as a place where they could practice their religion freely and create a better environment for their children.

The first group to migrate for religious freedom had already separated from the Church of England. The Separatists obtained financial backing from a group of London investors who had permission to establish a colony near the mouth of the Hudson River, a few hundred miles north of Jamestown. The investors recruited others to join the venture who were not members of the Separatist congregation. All 102 colonists would be required to work for the company for a certain length of time under a communal arrangement similar to the early Jamestown plan.*

In September 1620 they set sail from England aboard the *Mayflower*. Unlike the first Jamestown settlers, the group was composed mostly of families. They arrived in America in present-day Massachusetts, 200 miles north of their destination and outside the area granted to their sponsors. Some saw this as an opportunity to strike out on their own. The Separatists persuaded the other colonists to stay together and work with them to enact "just and equal laws...for the general good of the colony." Before disembarking they put their agreement in writing and signed the Mayflower Compact, an important document in America's progression toward self-government.

These colonists, Separatists and non-Separatists alike, are commonly referred to as the Pilgrims even though only the Separatists made the journey for religious reasons. The colony began in December 1620 at Plymouth, the site of an abandoned Indian village. Finding land already cleared of trees was a great benefit to the Pilgrims, but the winter was devastating nonetheless. Half their number died from disease and exposure.

Near the beginning of spring, an Indian walked into the settlement and surprised the Pilgrims by greeting them in English. Samoset had picked up bits of the language from English fishermen plying the waters off the northeast coast. Six days later he introduced another Indian to the Pilgrims. Squanto (or Tisquantum) spoke English fluently, having been kidnapped by an English explorer in 1614. He had made his way back to New England after five years only to find that his tribe and others along the coast had been decimated by disease. Squanto was invaluable as an interpreter. He showed the Plymouth colonists how Native Americans caught fish and eels and cultivated the soil to grow corn, beans, and squash.

The Pilgrims' leader, John Carver, died in April of 1621. William Bradford, chosen to take his place, would lead the Plymouth colony for 30 years.

In the fall, the Pilgrims marked their first harvest with three days of celebration and feasting with a hundred local Wampanoag Indians and their chief, Massasoit.[†] Working with Native Americans in Maine, the Pilgrims developed a profitable fur trade, particularly in beaver pelts.

In 1630 another group left England seeking religious freedom. Unlike the Pilgrims, the Puritans chose to remain members of the Church of England and purify it, albeit from afar. Their leader, John Winthrop, told them their colony in America would be "a city upon a hill" for all to see. They established the Massachusetts Bay Colony in and around Boston, 40 miles north of the Pilgrims in Plymouth. Boston was a better site, with a large deepwater harbor and navigable rivers into the interior.

The Massachusetts Bay colony, whose citizens were wealthier, better educated, and migrated in greater numbers than their Plymouth or Jamestown counterparts, progressed more rapidly. They formed a representative government but limited participation to male Puritans who adhered to strict religious standards. Colonial taxes were used to support the church and establish schools. Religious dissent was tolerated but within narrow boundaries.

The constraints of Puritan society and the need for better farmland compelled some colonists to start settlements elsewhere in Massachusetts. Roger Williams and Anne Hutchinson, banished for their beliefs, founded separate settlements that became part of a new colony: Rhode Island. Thomas Hooker led his congregation to land that became the Connecticut colony. Others branched out to present-day New Hampshire. In general, these breakaway colonies allowed greater religious freedom than Massachusetts Bay, established a clearer separation between religious and political affairs, and had fewer restrictions on who could vote or hold public office.

---

* *The Plymouth colonists would discontinue their communal economy after three years.*

† *The peace forged by Massasoit and the Pilgrims, although tenuous at times, lasted more than 50 years, but his son, Metacom (called King Philip by the colonists), would lead a war against the northeastern colonies of New England in 1675-76. During King Philip's War, a thousand colonists and 4,000 Native Americans were killed, including women and children on both sides. Of New England's 90 towns, 12 were completely destroyed and 40 others were damaged along with crops. Thousands of head of livestock were killed. Indian allies of the colonists helped defeat Metacom, but it was decades before the region fully recovered. Hundreds of Indians captured by the colonists were sold as slaves and shipped off to the Caribbean.*

7

THIRTEEN COLONIES

England's King Charles I granted Lord Baltimore the authority to establish a colony 200 miles north of Jamestown in 1632. Baltimore wanted his Maryland colony to be a refuge for fellow Catholics, who suffered discrimination at the hands of the Protestant majority in England.

In 1663 Charles II, recently restored to the English throne, rewarded eight loyal noblemen by granting them a vast tract of land between Virginia and Florida. The colony was named Carolina, from the Latin word for Charles. Rice became Carolina's main export.

The southern part of the colony grew more rapidly due in large measure to the excellent harbor at Charleston. The northern part, rimmed with barrier islands and shoals that were treacherous for ships, had the additional geographic disadvantage of extensive wetlands. In 1712 the colony was split into two separate entities, North Carolina and South Carolina.

Sandwiched between England's northern and southern possessions was a colony of the Netherlands, a Dutch-speaking country in Europe. Disregarding Dutch claims to the area, King Charles II bestowed the land on his brother, the duke of York.

In 1664 a small English fleet landed in New Amsterdam, the main Dutch settlement on Manhattan Island, at the mouth of the Hudson River. The unpopular Dutch governor, Peter Stuyvesant, was unable to muster support to resist the invaders and surrendered without a shot being fired. The settlement and the colony were renamed New York. The duke gave a portion of the territory to two English noblemen. That land became a separate colony named New Jersey.

To settle a debt owed to the Penn family, Charles II granted William Penn proprietary rights to land between New York and Maryland in 1681. Penn was greatly influenced by his Quaker faith and saw his Pennsylvania colony as a "holy experiment" where people of different races, religions, nationalities, and social classes could live together in harmony. Like Roger Williams of Rhode Island, William Penn respected native cultures and learned to converse with local Indians. He recognized their ownership of the land and purchased it from them. He was personally involved in laying out the city of Philadelphia, a name which means "brotherly love" in Greek. The duke of York increased Penn's holdings with land that became the Delaware colony.

In 1732 King George II granted James Oglethorpe and several other trustees a royal charter to establish the Georgia colony. The following year, Oglethorpe led the first group of settlers from England. Formed from land that had been part of South Carolina, this new colony would assist Carolina in quelling Indian attacks and act as a buffer against the Spanish in Florida, whose outpost at Saint Augustine predated Jamestown.

Oglethorpe had originally wanted Georgia to be a place where debtors languishing in English prisons could work to pay off their obligations and start a new life in America, but that plan was never implemented. The trustees did, however, provide passage and small farms to 1,800 poor Englishmen.

Britain now had 13 colonies in three regions along the East Coast:

New England	**Middle**	**Southern**
New Hampshire	New York	Maryland
Massachusetts	Pennsylvania	Virginia
Rhode Island	New Jersey	North Carolina
Connecticut	Delaware	South Carolina
		Georgia

Each colony had its own set of laws and a governing body of elected representatives with taxing authority, but colonists were still British subjects. The control exerted by Great Britain changed over time and varied depending on the colony.

8
NO TAXATION WITHOUT REPRESENTATION

While Britain was building up her colonies on the Eastern Seaboard of North America, France laid claim to an expanse of land in the interior stretching from Canada down to the Gulf of Mexico. Britain disputed part of the French claim and in 1754 went to war. The conflict is called the French and Indian War because various tribes fought alongside the French against the English, who had Indian allies of their own. With support from its colonies, Britain was victorious.

In the Treaty of 1763 that ended the war, France ceded its territory east of the Mississippi River to Great Britain. Spain, an ally of France, ceded Florida. French territory west of the Mississippi was ceded to Spain as compensation for the loss of Florida.

By this time, the population of the Thirteen Colonies had reached two million. Ninety-five percent of the people lived in rural areas, but Boston, New York, Philadelphia, and Charleston were thriving cities with busy ports.* The growing economy produced goods for sale within the colonies, to the West Indies,† and across the Atlantic and created a market of consumers needing goods from abroad.

After the French and Indian War, Britain tried to wield greater control over the Thirteen Colonies. The Royal Proclamation of 1763 prohibited colonists from venturing beyond the Appalachian Mountains into the territory recently acquired from France. Parliament, the supreme legislative body in Britain, banned colonial paper money and required the colonies to provide food, shelter, and other necessities to British soldiers stationed in America. The most irritating new policy was a stamp tax.

The debts incurred during the French and Indian War put a strain on the British treasury. To the British government, it seemed only fair that the colonies help pay for the support and protection they received from their mother country. The tax applied to printed material. Without a stamp, legal documents, such as deeds and wills, would not be valid; newspapers, pamphlets, and playing cards could not legally be sold; and advertisements were not allowed to be posted.

A storm of protest, which included violence, followed the announcement of this first direct tax on the colonists. They refused to pay it. The cry in America was "No taxation without representation!" Colonists were not going to accept taxes imposed on them without their consent and without colonial representatives in Parliament looking out for their interests and helping to make the laws. Without such representation, colonists had no say in how much they were taxed or how the taxes collected were spent.

Britain gave in and repealed the Stamp Act in 1766 but maintained the right to enact laws to govern and tax its colonies.

* *The largest cities in America were still small by European standards. In 1760 the population of Philadelphia was 19,000, Boston 16,000, New York 14,000, and Charleston 8,000. London boasted 700,000 residents and Paris 600,000.*

† *The islands of the Caribbean were known as the West Indies even though they had no geographic connection with the Indies in Asia (East Indies). Spain, France, the Netherlands, Denmark, and Britain all established colonies in the West Indies.*

9
MASSACRE and TEA PARTY
in BOSTON

The following year, 1767, Parliament passed the Townshend Acts, which levied taxes on English glass, paper, paint, and tea coming into America. Once again, colonists rejected Britain's right to tax them without representation. Protests were the most heated in Massachusetts. Britain dissolved the colony's representative assembly and sent soldiers, nicknamed redcoats, to Boston.

On a cold late-winter night in 1770, a crowd gathered in front of the customs house in Boston to harass a squad of redcoats. Colonists hurling snowballs, sticks, and chunks of ice knocked one of the soldiers to the ground. The redcoats fired into the crowd, killing five people. The incident, which became known as the Boston Massacre, outraged colonists. The British government tried to calm the situation by repealing most of the taxes imposed by the Townshend Acts, but the tax on tea was left in place.

In 1773 three English ships loaded with tea sailed into Boston Harbor. The colonial governor of Massachusetts, appointed by the king, demanded that the tea be unloaded and the tax be paid. The colonists balked. In the midst of the standoff, Samuel Adams and a group of revolutionaries, some masquerading as Indians, boarded the ships one evening and dumped all the tea into the harbor. They were cheered on by thousands of sympathetic colonists who came out to watch the Boston Tea Party.

Parliament met this blatant act of defiance by passing the Coercive Acts, also called the Intolerable Acts by the colonists. British authorities closed Boston Harbor, banned town meetings,* and extended the boundary of Quebec (a Canadian province also under British rule) south to the Ohio River, thus blocking westward expansion by some of the Thirteen Colonies.

Colonists responded by forming an intercolonial assembly that convened in Philadelphia in September of 1774. Delegates to the First Continental Congress declared the Coercive Acts null and void, called for a trade boycott with Britain, and encouraged the people of Massachusetts to take up arms for their defense. The Congress adjourned in October with plans to reconvene in May.

The First Continental Congress demonstrated that the colonies could come together and work out a unified response, but they did not seek independence from Great Britain. Most colonists wanted to remain English citizens. Others insisted that the time had come to break away. In a moving speech calling for revolution, Patrick Henry of Virginia said:

> Is life so dear, or peace so sweet, as to be purchased at the price of chains and slavery? Forbid it, Almighty God! I know not what course others may take; but as for me, give me liberty, or give me death!

---

* *In the villages typical of New England, town meetings were an example of direct democracy in America. Without intermediaries, residents voted for ordinances to govern their town.*

10
LEXINGTON and CONCORD

With their colonial assembly dissolved and town meetings banned, elected leaders in Massachusetts had to meet secretly. In preparation for the armed conflict that seemed increasingly likely, they organized a militia, or local civilian military force. Knowing they would have to react quickly to stand any chance against the powerful British army, the militia designated and trained certain members as minutemen, soldiers who would be ready to fight at a moment's notice.

Colonists monitored the activities of redcoats stationed in Boston and devised plans to quickly communicate their movements. If the troops deployed at night, colonial spies would use lamps to send a signal from the Old North Church, the tallest building in the city. One lamp would mean the redcoats were heading out on foot. Two lamps would mean they were being ferried across the harbor before beginning their march.

On a mild spring evening in 1775, the British began preparing boats to transport 700 soldiers. Quickly but silently the warning went out; two lamps were held up briefly in the belfry of the church steeple.

The colonists sprang into action. They knew the redcoats were headed for Concord, 20 miles away, where the colonial militia had been storing munitions. Paul Revere and William Dawes raced out on horseback. Taking different routes to reduce the possibility of both being captured, they spread the word that the redcoats were coming. Church bells, signal guns, beacon fires, drums, and additional messengers on horseback carried the warning swiftly throughout the countryside.

Revere and Dawes met up in Lexington, a town along the way, where a young doctor named Samuel Prescott joined them. The three men soon encountered a British patrol, which captured Revere. Dawes and Prescott managed to escape, but Dawes was thrown from his horse. Only Dr. Prescott made it to Concord, but the alarm had been raised, and colonists were coming out of their homes with gun in hand, ready to fight.

By sunrise the redcoats had traveled as far as Lexington. Seventy minutemen were waiting for them on the green. The British commander ordered the militia to disperse. And then a shot rang out. It is unclear who fired first, but a brief battle ensued that left eight minutemen dead and one of the redcoats wounded.

The British troops arrived in Concord later that morning. The militia had already moved the bulk of its military supplies, but what little the redcoats found they destroyed. They cut down and burned the town's liberty pole, a rallying point for anti-British protests.

The militia engaged the redcoats briefly at the North Bridge. Then in the afternoon, as the British began their return march, the colonists struck with full force, but not head-on. Instead, they fired from behind trees, houses, barns, and fences along the route. The size of the militia had grown to a few thousand men. The redcoats would have been wiped out had reinforcements from Boston not arrived. As it was, they sustained 300 casualties. The militia lost a hundred patriots on that day, April 19, 1775, the beginning of the Revolutionary War.

11
SECOND CONTINENTAL CONGRESS

News of the battles at Lexington and Concord spread quickly. Men from across New England gathered around Boston to join the fight. The situation brought a greater sense of urgency to the Continental Congress when, as planned, it reconvened in Philadelphia in May 1775 at the Pennsylvania State House, later called Independence Hall. Delegates to the Second Continental Congress, among the most distinguished leaders in the colonies, laid plans for their defense by creating the Continental Army. The initial recruits would come from the militias already fighting in Massachusetts. By unanimous vote, the Congress appointed George Washington of Virginia as commander-in-chief of the army.

Before Washington arrived in Massachusetts, a major battle took place across the harbor from Boston. The engagement is commonly known as the Battle of Bunker Hill, although most of the fighting occurred on the adjacent Breed's Hill, where colonists constructed makeshift fortifications of earth and wood. The redcoats set nearby Charlestown ablaze before trying to take the hill. The militia repelled two assaults but ran out of ammunition on the third and had to retreat. More than a hundred Americans died, but the British suffered much heavier casualties and lost many of their officers.

After General Washington assumed military command and organized the Continental Army, the enemy holed up in Boston for eight months. To break the stalemate, Washington ordered his men to erect fortifications and place artillery on Dorchester Heights, all in a single evening. From this peninsula overlooking Boston, the Continental Army could bombard British troops in the city and British ships in the harbor.*

At daybreak, the sixth anniversary of the Boston Massacre, the redcoats were astonished to see what the Continental Army had accomplished overnight and quickly realized the precarious position they were now in. They prepared to attack the American emplacements, but a violent storm made it impossible.

Word came from the British that they would leave Boston without burning the city if their evacuation was not impeded. American troops held their fire, and on March 17, 1776, redcoats and colonists loyal to the crown departed on ships bound for Nova Scotia. Victorious soldiers of the Continental Army moved into the liberated city.

In less than a year after the war began, the redcoats in Boston (the only British troops in the colonies at the time) were gone. Knowing they would return to America, General Washington and the army prepared for the next battles.

Meanwhile, a recent immigrant from England, Thomas Paine, published a 48-page pamphlet entitled *Common Sense*. It was widely read in the colonies and gave compelling reasons for severing ties with Great Britain. The Second Continental Congress was struggling to decide whether to take that drastic step or work toward reconciliation. The pamphlet and its popularity helped convince the Congress that a complete break was inevitable. Thirty-three-year-old Thomas Jefferson of Virginia, one of the youngest yet most gifted delegates, was given the task of writing a declaration of independence. The document would announce their decision and list 27 grievances that justified their actions.

* *The artillery placed on Dorchester Heights came from Fort Ticonderoga in upstate New York. The British had given up the fort the previous year after Ethan Allen, leader of a New England militia, demanded their surrender "in the name of the Great Jehovah and the Continental Congress." General Washington put Henry Knox, a bookseller by trade, in charge of hauling the 60 tons of equipment to Boston across 300 miles of mountains, lakes, rivers, snow, and mud, a remarkable logistical feat that took six weeks.*

12
DECLARATION of INDEPENDENCE

On July 4, 1776, the Second Continental Congress adopted the Declaration of Independence as the official announcement of the separation of the Thirteen Colonies from Great Britain. Americans have celebrated the Fourth of July as Independence Day ever since. The formal parchment copy of the Declaration, on display in the National Archives, was signed first by John Hancock, the leader of the Congress. His signature was so prominent and impressive that his name became a synonym for signature. There were 56 signers in all.

The Declaration of Independence set forth founding principles that have been a guide and inspiration ever since. It begins:

> When in the Course of human events, it becomes necessary for one people to dissolve the political bands which have connected them with another, and to assume among the powers of the earth, the separate and equal station to which the Laws of Nature and of Nature's God entitle them, a decent respect to the opinions of mankind requires that they should declare the causes which impel them to the separation.

> We hold these truths to be self-evident, that all men are created equal, that they are endowed by their Creator with certain unalienable* Rights, that among these are Life, Liberty and the pursuit of Happiness – That to secure these rights, Governments are instituted among Men, deriving their just powers from the consent of the governed – That whenever any Form of Government becomes destructive of these ends, it is the Right of the People to alter or to abolish it, and to institute new Government, laying its foundation on such principles and organizing its powers in such form, as to them shall seem most likely to effect their Safety and Happiness.

The final paragraph states:

> We, therefore, the Representatives of the United States of America, in General Congress, Assembled, appealing to the Supreme Judge of the world for the rectitude of our intentions, do, in the Name, and by Authority of the good People of these Colonies, solemnly publish and declare, That these United Colonies are, and of Right ought to be Free and Independent States; that they are Absolved from all Allegiance to the British Crown, and that all political connection between them and the State of Great Britain, is and ought to be totally dissolved... And for the support of this Declaration, with a firm reliance on the protection of divine Providence, we mutually pledge to each other our Lives, our Fortunes and our sacred Honor.

The colonies were now states joined together as a new nation. That system of government, with a central authority and constituent states exercising power over the same body of citizens, is known as federalism. The 13 red and white stripes on the American flag represent the original states. The concept of a union of states is also expressed in the motto, *E Pluribus Unum*, a 13-letter Latin phrase that appears on U.S. currency and means "out of many, one."[†]

General Washington ordered that the Declaration of Independence be read to the Continental Army. He told them he hoped "that this important event will serve as a fresh incentive to every officer, and soldier, to act with fidelity and courage, as knowing that now the peace and safety of his country depends, under God, solely on the success of our arms."

* *absolute, inherent, sacred, incapable of being transferred*

† *The phrase "In God We Trust," which first appeared on U.S. currency in 1864, became the official national motto in 1956.*

13
COULD AMERICA DEFEAT BRITAIN ?

Declaring independence did not make it so. England was not going to give up valuable colonies without a fight. The monarchy and the Parliament took action to crush the rebellion.

Americans made the decision to take up arms despite the enemy's considerable advantages. Britain controlled a global empire and was the dominant economic and military power in the world. It could marshal hundreds of ships and tens of thousands of well-trained and well-equipped soldiers and sailors.

America, on the other hand, had only a fledgling navy and had difficulty organizing and maintaining a national army. Citizens identified more with their local area and state than with the large nation of which they were now a part. The military had to rely on volunteers because the Continental Congress did not have authority to compel men to serve. Those who were willing to fight were often poorly armed, poorly trained, and lacked adequate food, clothing, and shelter. Procuring supplies and money to pay the soldiers was difficult without a strong central government.

The nascent United States was not without strengths, however. Many of its soldiers and commanders had proven themselves in battle during the French and Indian War and in the opening clashes of the Revolution. The war for independence would be fought on terrain more familiar to American soldiers than to the British. And the U.S. would receive support from France and Spain. But the biggest advantage for Americans was that they were fighting for their homes, their way of life, and for the ideals of liberty, independence, and a new nation. Nevertheless, a sizable number of colonists, possibly more than 400,000 out of a total population of 2½ million, maintained allegiance to the British king, George III, and were labeled Loyalists or Tories.

⊷◍◍◍◍◍◍⊷

14
GENERAL WASHINGTON
and the CONTINENTAL ARMY

Just a few months after evacuating Boston, the British military returned to America with a massive show of force to regain control over the colonies. On July 2, 1776, two days before the Declaration of Independence was adopted, 32,000 British soldiers and more than 400 ships and their crews began arriving in New York Harbor. The Continental Army and state militias, a combined force of only 19,000, were nearly overwhelmed at the Battle of Long Island. Washington and his men retreated as far as the East River, where they were trapped. A final assault by the redcoats would have destroyed the vulnerable, rain-soaked American troops and probably ended the war, but the British commander dallied.

Seizing the opportunity, General Washington assembled every available sailboat, rowboat, and barge during the night and quietly directed the ferrying of his army, including horses and artillery, across the mile-wide river to Manhattan. The direction of the wind aided the American flotilla and kept the British fleet from sailing upriver to block an escape. The last regiments were still awaiting passage when daylight threatened to expose the ongoing evacuation, but an unusually thick fog rolled in and remained after sunrise, concealing American troops from the enemy's view until all had made it across. Washington was the last to leave.

The Continental Army was retreating again a few weeks later when the redcoats captured Manhattan and then advanced toward Pennsylvania. The Continental Congress relocated from Philadelphia to Baltimore, Maryland. By December of 1776, after a year and a half of fighting, the Revolution seemed doomed. Most of the soldiers in the Continental Army had enlisted for only 12 months and those commitments were set to expire on December 31.

In this dark period, Thomas Paine encouraged Americans with the words:

> These are the times that try men's souls. The summer soldier and the sunshine patriot will, in this crisis, shrink from the service of their country; but he that stands it now, deserves the love and thanks of man and woman. Tyranny, like hell, is not easily conquered; yet we have this consolation with us, that the harder the conflict, the more glorious the triumph.

Americans were also inspired by the courage of Nathan Hale, a 21-year-old Yale graduate and a captain in the Continental Army. He volunteered to spy on the enemy but was captured. As he was about to be hanged by the redcoats, he reputedly said, "I only regret that I have but one life to lose for my country."

The outlook improved dramatically before the end of the year. On December 25 the Continental Army was camped near the Delaware River. On the opposite side of the river, Hessian (German) mercenaries fighting for the British held the town of Trenton, New Jersey. The Hessians did not suspect any danger. Not only was it Christmas, but the weather was bitterly cold and stormy, snow covered the ground, and floating ice in the river made a crossing by the Americans highly unlikely.

Under the cover of darkness, Washington and the army slipped across the Delaware in boats and barges and made their way to Trenton. At eight o'clock the next morning they struck, catching the enemy off guard. More than a hundred Hessian soldiers were killed or wounded in the one-hour rout, and 900 were taken prisoner. American troops suffered few casualties. Elated with the success of his risky plan, Washington remarked to one of his officers, "This is a glorious day for our country."

After General Washington persuaded soldiers in the Continental Army to extend their enlistments beyond the end of the year, he led them in a successful assault on British troops at Princeton, New Jersey, in early January. These stunning back-to-back victories boosted American morale. New recruits swelled the ranks of the army and were willing to enlist for the long term, either three years or the duration of the war.

VALLEY FORGE and SARATOGA

In July of 1777, 15,000 redcoats sailed out of New York bound for the Chesapeake Bay. They disembarked in Maryland and marched toward Philadelphia. When the Continental Army failed to stop them at the Battle of Brandywine, the Congress had to flee the city again. Following another defeat, at nearby Germantown, George Washington led 12,000 troops to Valley Forge to take up winter quarters.

The Valley Forge encampment, 20 miles from the British army occupying Philadelphia, stretched for five square miles along the Schuylkill River. It would be the Continental Army's base for the next six months, through both winter and spring. Washington had the soldiers construct small log cabins for their lodging. Two thousand of the simple structures were built and they provided a modicum of comfort, but the conditions were still harsh. Food, clothing, blankets, and shoes were in short supply, and illness was widespread. Washington pressed the Continental Congress and the state governments for assistance in providing for his men. Aid of a different sort came from an unlikely source.

Friedrich von Steuben, a former officer in the Prussian* military, arrived at Valley Forge and offered to help train the Continental Army. He was appalled at the conditions and said no European army would have held together under such circumstances. General Washington gladly accepted his assistance.

Von Steuben did not speak English. His native language was German, but he also spoke French, as did some of the officers on Washington's staff. The translation of Von Steuben's profanity-laced instructions from French to English was often comical to the troops, but he taught them the essentials of military drill and helped transform the Continental Army into a disciplined fighting force. His insistence on proper sanitation was also invaluable.

Amid the hardships, soldiers at Valley Forge were encouraged by the far-reaching effects of a key battle won by other American troops 300 miles to the north. The British had launched an offensive out of Canada to cut off New England from the other states. They recaptured Fort Ticonderoga, but their advance stalled due to a lack of supplies and a numerical disadvantage against American regular troops and militias. In October of 1777 British General John Burgoyne and the 6,000 redcoats under his command surrendered at Saratoga, New York.

The defeat of such a large British army raised the hopes of Americans more than any previous victory and secured the northern states against British attacks out of Canada. Most important, it convinced the French that the U.S. could prevail over England, their centuries-old foe. After the Battle of Saratoga, France officially entered the war as America's ally. In addition to the money and munitions it was already supplying, France would now also provide soldiers and a navy.

Prussia was a European power in what is now northern Germany and Poland.

16
YORKTOWN

The British embarked on a major military campaign in the Southern states in 1778. It went badly for American forces in the beginning. After Savannah, Georgia, fell to the redcoats, the United States suffered its worst defeat of the war when 5,500 troops surrendered another port city: Charleston, South Carolina.

In New York a disaster was narrowly averted. Benedict Arnold, a hero at the Battle of Saratoga, was the commander of West Point. This strategic fort on the Hudson River had recently been established as the Continental Army's headquarters. The fort's defenses were engineered by Polish patriot Thaddeus Kosciuszko. Arnold made plans to hand over the fort to the redcoats in exchange for a large sum. The plot was foiled when his British accomplice was caught with documents related to the conspiracy hidden under his clothing. The papers were turned over to the Continental Army along with the British spy, who was hanged. Benedict Arnold escaped to the enemy occupying New York City before he could be arrested. Given the rank of general in the British army, Arnold was soon fighting against his former countrymen. His name would become synonymous with treason and betrayal.

The state of affairs in the South improved after General Washington assigned military command of the region to Nathanael Greene, one of America's most able generals. Greene's forces scored a victory at the Battle of Cowpens in South Carolina in January 1781, then drove the redcoats northward out of the Carolinas and into Virginia. The British commander in the South, General Charles Cornwallis, established his base of operations at Yorktown, Virginia, on the banks of the York River, and unwittingly set the stage for a decisive battle.

General Washington was planning to attack the British stronghold of New York City when he learned that Cornwallis was at Yorktown and the French fleet commanded by Admiral de Grasse was sailing up from the Caribbean toward Virginia. Washington quickly mobilized both U.S. and French forces to converge on Yorktown. British ships set sail from New York to evacuate Cornwallis and his army. Victory largely depended on which ships arrived first. Fortunately, they were French.

The French fleet blocked the British navy from rescuing Cornwallis by sea. American and French troops led by Washington, von Steuben, and the French commanders Rochambeau and Lafayette sealed off overland escape routes. With nowhere to turn, Cornwallis's army of 8,000 surrendered on October 19, 1781, after a month-long siege. Their defeat convinced Great Britain that the war was lost.

17
ARTICLES of CONFEDERATION

Fighting continued sporadically for two years after the Battle of Yorktown as British troops and Loyalists left the U.S. and diplomats worked out a peace treaty in France. The Treaty of Paris negotiated by Benjamin Franklin, John Adams, and John Jay brought a formal end to the Revolutionary War in 1783. Britain ceded not only the 370,000 square miles of territory within the borders of the 13 original states, but also the 475,000 square miles that stretched westward to the Mississippi River. The young nation celebrated as the last remaining redcoats sailed out of New York City on November 25, and General Washington and soldiers of the Continental Army entered.

At that moment George Washington was the most powerful person in the country, but having fulfilled his commission as commander-in-chief of the army, he promptly tendered his resignation to the Congress meeting in Annapolis, Maryland. This act demonstrated his conviction that the military was subordinate to civil authority. A private citizen once again, the 51-year-old Washington rode more than 40 miles on horseback to his Virginia estate at Mount Vernon, arriving in time to spend Christmas there for the first time in eight years.

With the old British government thrown off, the country could now concentrate on establishing permanent American government institutions. This was much easier at the state level because states were largely autonomous and their predecessor colonial governments had long histories. Creating a national government presented a host of challenges. The Continental Congress had been a provisional government concerned primarily with prosecuting the war. The first permanent central government was created in 1781 with ratification of the

Articles of Confederation. The institution thus created had just one branch, the Congress.

The Confederation Congress oversaw the successful conclusion of the war and a peace treaty with Britain. It made substantial progress toward settling the nation's debts, established government departments (war, foreign affairs, finance, post office), and built up a staff of employees (clerks, secretaries, translators) to help run the day-to-day affairs, including during times when Congress was not in session. The government also formulated guidelines for the survey, sale, and governance of western territories, which were to be placed under federal, not state, control. After meeting certain criteria, new states would be formed out of the territories instead of simply enlarging the existing states.

On the whole, though, the institution created by the Articles of Confederation proved inadequate. It was weak by design. The Founders did not want to replace the powerful central government of Great Britain with one of their own making for fear it would take away the liberties they had fought to secure. Consequently, laws enacted by the Confederation Congress were little more than recommendations.

Since Congress lacked the authority to enforce its measures, it had to rely on the goodwill of the states. This created many problems, not the least of which was the raising of revenue. Taxation was the purview of state and local governments; the Articles granted the national government no such authority. The country's debts from the war and the expenses of the federal government were to be paid out of a treasury funded by the states, but states could not be forced to pay their share, and their payments were in arrears. A central government without sufficient, timely, and independent funding could not be effective.

Under the Articles of Confederation, the federal government had little power to regulate domestic or foreign trade. Congress entered into treaties of commerce with other countries but could not compel the states to abide by the provisions. Each state imposed its own import and export taxes and restrictions. The nation did not have a stable and uniform currency. Seven states issued their own currency.

The Articles had additional flaws. Each state was allotted one vote on legislation considered by the Congress. This gave states with small populations as much power in the government as large states. Legislation on such important matters as raising a military force, entering into treaties, borrowing money, and making expenditures required a two-thirds vote rather than a simple majority. A unanimous vote was required to amend the Articles. Congress could not override a state law.

Delegates to Congress served one-year terms up to a maximum of three terms in a six-year period, which created a problem of continuity in the government. Compounding matters, delegates often showed their state's indifference toward the institution by staying home instead of attending congressional sessions.

The Confederation Congress was unsuccessful in persuading or coercing Spain to grant Americans free navigation of the Mississippi River. It was also unable to compel Britain to evacuate its outposts on U.S. soil along the Canadian border, a stipulation of the Treaty of Paris.

In 1786, only three years after the end of the Revolutionary War, an armed uprising broke out in Massachusetts over high taxes. The rebels took over courthouses to prevent judges from ordering the seizure of their property to satisfy delinquent assessments. Twelve hundred disaffected citizens led by Daniel Shays threatened a federal arsenal. The state appealed to the national government for assistance, but Congress lacked the wherewithal to help.

A former officer in the Continental Army suggested to George Washington that he use his influence to help put down the insurrection. Mortified by this violent challenge to law and order, Washington replied, "Influence is no government. Let us have one by which our lives, liberties, and properties will be secured."

Many in Britain expected the United States to collapse and viewed the civil unrest in Massachusetts and other states as proof that Americans were incapable of governing themselves. Shays's Rebellion was finally quelled in February 1787 by a state militia funded by Massachusetts merchants. The inability of the Confederation Congress to deal with the crisis underscored the desperate need for a stronger central government and a more effective framework.

18
THE CONSTITUTION

To address the weaknesses of the Articles of Confederation, a convention was planned for May 1787 in Philadelphia. George Washington's decision to attend added to the prestige of the gathering and attracted other prominent and able men. It was "an assembly of demigods" according to Thomas Jefferson, who was serving abroad as ambassador to France. Every state but Rhode Island sent representatives.

Delegates to the Constitutional Convention, meeting in the same room in Independence Hall where the Declaration had been adopted, realized the enormity of their task and what was at stake. Virginia delegate George Mason wrote, "The revolt from Great Britain and the formations of our new governments at that time were nothing compared to the great business now before us." He predicted that "the happiness or misery of millions yet unborn" would be affected by their work.

The first order of business was to select someone to preside over the proceedings. The convention chose the man who had led the Continental Army to victory and was respected by all: George Washington. The participants then agreed to keep their deliberations strictly confidential until their work was completed. This was more conducive to open and frank discussion of the issues and made it easier for delegates to change positions. It is doubtful that the work of the Constitutional Convention could have been accomplished if delegates had divulged information or if the meetings had been open to the public or the press.

From the outset there was general agreement that the central government should be strengthened. The debate revolved around three fundamental questions:

How strong should the federal government be?

How should it be structured?

How should each state be represented?

Instead of merely revising the Articles of Confederation, as Congress and the states had instructed, the delegates in Philadelphia set about creating a completely new document. James Madison is called the "father of the Constitution" because he wrote the Virginia Plan, the blueprint or basis for debate.

The issues were complicated and the delegates represented diverse interests and constituencies. They had to compromise for the process to be fair and to reach a consensus. Working every day except Sunday, they debated the important matters and resolved differences. On some points there were sharp disagreements. There were days when the convention seemed destined for failure, but the delegates persisted.

After four months of meetings they agreed on a final draft, written primarily by Pennsylvania delegate Gouverneur Morris. On Monday, September 17, 1787, the delegates met for the last time to sign the document. George Washington went first. Thirty-eight others came forward by state. Benjamin Franklin is said to have wept when he signed.

The average age of the signers of the Constitution was 44. More than a third were in their twenties and thirties. At 81, Franklin of Pennsylvania was by far the oldest.

In only four pages, the Constitution laid out a new form of government. The Preamble states the purpose:

WE THE PEOPLE of the United States, in Order to form a more perfect Union, establish Justice, insure domestic Tranquility, provide for the common defence, promote the general Welfare, and secure the Blessings of Liberty to ourselves and our Posterity, do ordain and establish this Constitution for the United States of America.

The signing in Philadelphia did not make the Constitution the law of the land. As specified by the document itself, it first had to be approved by the states, but not by their respective legislatures. Instead, delegates chosen by the people would decide the matter in special state conventions. Mindful of the difficulty in reaching unanimity, the Framers stipulated that the Constitution would be binding upon all ratifying states when two-thirds of the state conventions voted in favor. Approval would have to be unconditional. No amendments were allowed before ratification.

The Constitution was debated in all 13 states, and the outcome was not at all certain. In a series of 85 essays – known collectively as *The Federalist Papers* – Alexander Hamilton, James Madison, and John Jay explained the proposed Constitution and made compelling arguments for its ratification.

Delaware was the first state to vote in favor. One by one, other states followed. In June 1788 New Hampshire became the ninth state to vote for ratification. With the two-thirds requirement met, the Constitution became law. By 1790 all 13 states had ratified the document.

19
THREE BRANCHES

The seven articles of the Constitution laid out a structure with power derived "from the consent of the governed," divided among three branches, and limited in its jurisdiction over states and individual citizens but strong enough for the government to be effective. The Constitution is the supreme law of the land. No federal statute may contradict it. The Constitution, federal laws and regulations, and U.S. treaties take precedence over conflicting state provisions. The national government is a higher power than any state government or group of states.

The Constitution guarantees to every state a republican form of government and protection from invasion and domestic violence. Citizens are entitled to the same "privileges and immunities" in all the states but may not flee to another state to escape criminal justice. The Constitution prohibits a religious test for holding federal office and bars the taxing of a state's exports. States may not print money or enter into treaties with foreign countries and are required to recognize the acts of the other states (give "full faith and credit").

The first and lengthiest article of the Constitution is devoted to the *LEGISLATIVE BRANCH*, or Congress, the predominant branch of the government.* Congress writes the laws, including those controlling federal revenues and expenditures. The legislature is empowered to levy taxes, borrow money, regulate the monetary system, regulate commerce among the states and with foreign nations, raise an army and navy, declare war, and use the military to suppress insurrections and enforce federal law.

Congress is bicameral. The two chambers are the House of Representatives and the Senate. The manner in which states would be represented in these two bodies was the most divisive issue at the Constitutional Convention. Large states, such as Virginia, favored population as the basis for representation. New Jersey and other small states lobbied for equal representation for each state, a continuation of the Articles of Confederation model. The agreement that overcame the impasse has been called the Great Compromise. State representation would be equal in the Senate and by population in the House.

To achieve proportional representation in the House of Representatives, the country is divided into congressional districts within each state. Each district, roughly the same size in terms of population,[†] is represented by one congressman in the House. States with larger populations have more congressional districts. California, the most populous state, currently has 53 congressional districts and, therefore, 53 seats in the House of Representatives. Delaware, Alaska, and five other states with relatively small populations have only one congressional district and one representative, the constitutional minimum for a state. All House seats come up for election every two years.[‡]

Since state populations fluctuate, the Constitution requires that a census, or count of the country's population, be taken every 10 years. States with large population increases relative to the other states gain one or more seats in the House of Representatives, while states with large population decreases lose seats. When a state's apportionment changes, say from four congressional districts to five, the district boundaries within that state have to be redrawn. In most states, governors and state legislators have the primary responsibility for redistricting.

In the Senate, representation is equal. Every state, regardless of its size in land area or population, has two senators. They represent all the citizens of a state. Senators are elected for six-year terms, but they do not all face reelection in the same year. Every two years a third of the Senate comes up for reelection. Likewise, a state's two senators do not both face reelection in the same year. Staggering senatorial elections in this manner promotes continuity in the Congress.[§]

Either chamber may initiate legislation, but revenue (tax) bills must originate in the House of Representatives. A quorum (a majority of the members of a chamber) must be present before a bill is put to a vote. Most legislation passes with a simple majority of those present voting in favor.[¶] The vice-president may cast a tie-breaking vote in the Senate.

If the House and Senate pass different versions of a bill and compromise is possible, members from both chambers are selected to work out the differences in a conference committee. The compromise bill must be voted on by both chambers. Only after an identical bill passes in both the House and the Senate does legislation move on to the White House for approval.

The *EXECUTIVE BRANCH*, described in Article II of the Constitution, is headed by a single president who, along with a vice-president, is elected every four years and represents all the people. The president must be a natural-born citizen. The highest official in the government, he enforces federal laws and exercises powers set forth by the Constitution and Congress. The president approves or rejects bills passed by the legislature and may also recommend legislation. He is commander-in-chief of the military.

The president chooses a cabinet to help run the executive branch. Cabinet members manage various departments and are all given the title of secretary, except for the head of the Justice Department, whose title is attorney general. There are currently 15 cabinet-level executive departments: Defense, State, Treasury, Justice, Interior, Agriculture, Commerce, Labor, Health & Human Services, Housing & Urban Development, Transportation, Energy, Education, Veterans Affairs, and Homeland Security.

The third branch of the central government, the *JUDICIAL BRANCH*, consists of the federal courts. Their jurisdiction, or authority to hear a case, is defined by Article III of the Constitution and by federal law. Federal courts hear cases involving the Constitution, federal laws and regulations, and treaties. They also take up controversies between the states, between citizens of different states, and between American citizens and foreigners.

In the federal judiciary there are three main levels: district courts, circuit courts (courts of appeals), and the Supreme Court. The Constitution created the Supreme Court and authorized the legislative branch to create the lower federal courts.

U.S. district courts are trial courts and courts of original jurisdiction, meaning they hear cases at their inception. Every state has at least one federal district court; the most populous states have four. In district court cases, verdicts are rendered by either judges or juries. At all other levels in the federal court system, only judges decide cases.

A ruling by a district court may be appealed to its respective regional circuit court. For example, the Seventh Circuit hears appeals from district courts in Illinois, Indiana, and Wisconsin. A decision by a circuit court may be appealed to the highest federal court, the Supreme Court, which also has original jurisdiction over a small range of cases.

Federal judges are not elected. They are nominated by the president and, with the "advice and consent" of the Senate, appointed for life. Nominees must be confirmed by the Senate before they can sit on the bench. Congress determines the number of judges at all levels of the federal judiciary.

Judicial Level	Number of Courts	Number of Judgeships
District Court	94	678
Circuit Court (Court of Appeals)	13	179
Supreme Court	1	9

Courts do not initiate lawsuits. They interpret and apply the law in adjudicating cases brought before them. Rulings by the judiciary frequently rely on precedent, or how relevant cases were decided in the past.

States have their own constitutions and governments that mirror the structure of the federal government. Executive, legislative, and judicial branches at the state level operate in their jurisdictions in a similar manner to their counterparts at the national level. There are state senators, state representatives, and state judges. The chief executive of a state carries the title of governor. Most legal disputes in the country are handled in state and local courts.

* *The three branches have different functions and cannot be equal or "co-equal."*

† *Originally, there was to be one representative for every 30,000 inhabitants. In the 2010 census apportionment, the average district population was 710,767.*

‡ *An act of Congress signed by President William Howard Taft in 1911 capped the total number of congressmen in the House of Representatives at 435.*

§ *Senators were originally chosen by their respective state legislatures. That provision of the Constitution was changed in 1913. The 17th Amendment established senatorial elections by the direct vote of citizens of each state.*

¶ *Controversial bills in the Senate typically need 60 votes to pass. According to Senate rules, if the majority is any less, a senator in the minority can filibuster, a parliamentary procedure that delays or prevents passage of a bill. House rules do not permit filibusters.*

CHECKS and BALANCES

The Framers of the Constitution limited the power of the federal government by dividing its functions – executive, legislative, and judicial – among three branches. The separation of powers is safeguarded by checks and balances built into the Constitution to minimize the risk that one of the three branches might take sole control of the government. These provisions give each branch a degree of leverage over the other two. Some checks and balances have already been mentioned. The following illustrates how they may be applied to legislation.

After a bill is passed by Congress, it is sent to the White House. If the president approves of the legislation, he signs it into law. If he disapproves, he can veto the bill. This action sends the bill back to Congress, where it dies or is once again put to a vote. If two-thirds of the legislators in each chamber (assuming they reach a quorum) vote in favor, the veto is overridden and the bill becomes law despite the president's objection.

Once a bill becomes law, the judicial branch can determine the effect of the law by ruling on relevant cases brought before the court. In such lawsuits a federal court may strike down the law as unconstitutional. This, in effect, nullifies the law and makes it unenforceable.*

Additional checks and balances are:

- The president has to rely on Congress for funding.
- Treaties negotiated with other countries and signed by the president do not become the law of the land and binding without the concurrence of two-thirds of the Senate.
- The president can exempt a citizen from criminal punishment. A presidential pardon can be granted before or after a trial.
- Cabinet secretaries nominated by the president must receive Senate confirmation before they can serve.
- Congress can impeach the president, judges, or other federal officials and remove them from office if they are deemed unfit to serve.

The ultimate power in a republic, and the greatest check and balance, rests with citizens who vote for officials who direct the affairs of the government.

The Constitution does not expressly give this authority to federal courts. Judicial review is assumed to be an implied power. In 1803 the Supreme Court's landmark ruling in Marbury v. Madison marked the first time the judiciary declared a law enacted by Congress and the president to be unconstitutional.

PRESIDENT WASHINGTON and the BILL OF RIGHTS

After the states ratified the Constitution, federal elections were held. As expected, George Washington was elected the nation's first president. The new government convened for the first time in 1789 in New York City. Bringing the Constitution to life in working institutions of effective government for a population of four million was a monumental task.* President Washington and the other leaders were keenly aware that everything they did would set precedents and give direction to their successors.

Notwithstanding the constraints that were in place, the early leaders were concerned that a federal government as powerful as the one created by the Constitution might infringe upon personal liberties and states' rights. To explicitly guarantee certain fundamental freedoms, rights, and protections, the first Congress passed ten amendments to the Constitution that were subsequently ratified by the states. They are known collectively as the Bill of Rights.

Amendment 1 prohibits the establishment of a national religion and guarantees the free exercise of religion. It guarantees freedom of speech, freedom of the press, the right to assemble peaceably, and the right to petition the government for a redress of grievances.

Amendment 2 guarantees the right to bear arms.

Amendment 3 prohibits the military from forcibly using private homes for lodging.

Amendment 4 protects against unreasonable searches and seizures.

Amendment 5 guarantees the right to due process of law. It protects a citizen from being tried twice for the same crime and from having to testify against oneself. It guarantees fair compensation for private property taken for public use, a process known as eminent domain.

Amendment 6 guarantees the right to a speedy and public trial by an impartial jury in criminal prosecutions. The accused is also guaranteed the right to the assistance of an attorney.

Amendment 7 guarantees the right to a jury trial in certain civil cases.

Amendment 8 protects against cruel and unusual punishment and excessive fines or bails.

Amendments 9 and 10 reserve to the states or the people all rights and powers not enumerated by the Constitution and delegated to the federal government.

Amending the Constitution is a two-step process of congressional approval and state ratification; the president is not directly involved. A proposed amendment must first pass by a two-thirds majority in both houses of Congress.[†] It is then presented to the state legislatures or to special state conventions for ratification. If three-fourths of the states vote in favor, the amendment is adopted and becomes binding throughout the country. The Constitution has been amended 27 times, most recently in 1992 over the issue of congressional pay raises.

* *According to the latest census, the nation's population in 2010 was 309 million, a 10 percent increase over the 281 million counted in the previous census in 2000.*

† *Two-thirds of the state legislatures may call a convention to propose amendments, but this alternative method allowed by Article V of the Constitution has never been implemented.*

22
POLITICAL PARTIES, WASHINGTON, D.C.,
and the LOUISIANA PURCHASE

Political parties are civic organizations whose objective is to gain power in government. They strive to choose the best candidates from their membership to compete for elective office against candidates from opposing parties. The Constitution makes no mention of political parties, but it was not long before two parties emerged with different visions for the future of the country. The Federalists, led by Alexander Hamilton, believed a strong central government was necessary for the United States to grow as a commercial empire. The Democratic-Republicans viewed the nation as an agricultural republic and resisted efforts to strengthen the federal government at the expense of states' rights. They were led by Thomas Jefferson.*

In 1790 the federal government relocated from New York to Philadelphia until a permanent capital city could be built. A site along the Potomac River was selected and named Washington, D.C. (District of Columbia).[†] By the year 1800, construction on the Capitol building and the White House was far enough along for the government to move to the new capital. John Adams of Massachusetts, who succeeded George Washington, was the first president to reside in the executive mansion.

The territory claimed by the United States extended only as far west as the Mississippi River, the nation's longest river. That waterway, with the port of New Orleans near its mouth, was an important channel of commerce for the new republic. Most of the land between the Mississippi and the Rocky Mountains was known as Louisiana and was largely uncharted. France had laid claim to the territory in 1682 but ceded it to Spain in 1763 after the French and Indian War.

In 1800, France reacquired Louisiana through a secret treaty with Spain. After the deal came to light, Thomas Jefferson, the nation's third president, sent ambassadors to France with an offer to purchase New Orleans, a vital hub for Americans transferring cargo to and from ocean-going vessels. Surprisingly, the French emperor, Napoleon, was willing to sell not just the city, but all of Louisiana. The Louisiana Purchase, an acquisition of 530 million acres, doubled the size of the country in 1803 for only $15 million, or less than 3¢ an acre.

President Jefferson was eager to know more about the newly acquired territory and what lay beyond it. He appointed his secretary, Meriwether Lewis, who was also a captain in the army, to organize and lead a military unit known as the Corps of Discovery. Their mission was to map the area, conduct scientific research, evaluate the land's mineral deposits and fertility, find the Northwest Passage to the Pacific Ocean, and establish peaceful relations with the Native Americans and become acquainted with their cultures. Lewis chose William Clark, his former commanding officer in the military, to help lead the venture.

In 1804 the Corps of Discovery left St. Louis and headed up the Missouri River. In present-day North Dakota a French-Canadian fur trapper, his Indian wife, Sacagawea, and their infant son joined the exploratory expedition. The presence of a woman and her child was perceived by Indians encountered on the trip as an indication that the 30-member party, made up mostly of soldiers, meant no harm. Sacagawea served as an interpreter in negotiations to obtain horses from her native Shoshone tribe, and her knowledge of edible wild plants was beneficial when provisions ran low.

The epic journey of Lewis and Clark lasted 28 months and covered 8,000 miles. They did not find a Northwest Passage, but the specimens they brought back in 1806 and their maps and detailed journals describing the land and recounting their experiences provided ample evidence of the expedition's success. It sparked the imagination of Americans and gave them a sense of the adventure to be found in the West.

---

* *Various political parties have come and gone since the nation's founding. For more than 150 years, there have been two major political parties in the United States: the Democratic Party, symbolized by a donkey, and the Republican Party (also known as the Grand Old Party, or GOP), symbolized by an elephant.*

† *Columbia (derived from Columbus) is a female figure first used in colonial times to symbolize America. Later she also came to represent, more specifically, the United States. Her image has appeared on U.S. coins and stamps.*

23
THE DAWN'S EARLY LIGHT and BARBARY PIRATES

Relations with England, tenuous following the Revolutionary War, deteriorated after 1800 to the point that there were again calls for military action. American settlers along the northern border accused the British in Canada of supplying arms to Indians and inciting them to attack. The prospect of acquiring territory in Canada and Florida was also put forward as a justification to fight, but Britain's provocations at sea were the main catalyst.

Already at war with France, Britain imposed a blockade of continental Europe and seized American merchant ships that ignored the restriction. Britain also stepped up its policy of impressment, the forcing of sailors abducted from American ships to serve in the Royal Navy. Some of the sailors were British deserters, but others were U.S. citizens by birth or through naturalization, which the British did not recognize. They regarded men born in England as English subjects for life and, therefore, obligated to serve in the British military. "Once an Englishman, always an Englishman."

The United States declared war on Great Britain in 1812. The low point came two years later when redcoats marched into Washington, D.C., and set fire to the White House, the Capitol, the Library of Congress, and other government buildings. A rare tornado and a violent thunderstorm did further damage but also put out the fires and hastened the departure of the enemy troops. British forces sailed up the Chesapeake Bay intent on taking the city of Baltimore. Fort McHenry, situated at the entrance to Baltimore Harbor, stood in their way.

As the British bombarded the fort through the night, Francis Scott Key, an American lawyer, watched from a ship nearby. The federal government had sent him to negotiate the release of a prisoner being held on an English vessel. He secured the man's freedom but was detained until after the battle. Early the next day, Key saw the U.S. flag still flying over Fort McHenry. Inspired by the successful defense of the fort, he wrote a poem that was set to a popular tune of the day. "The Star-Spangled Banner" became a well-known patriotic song in America.* The first of four stanzas reads:

> Oh say, can you see, by the dawn's early light,
> What so proudly we hailed at the twilight's last gleaming?
> Whose broad stripes and bright stars, through the perilous fight,
> O'er the ramparts[†] we watched, were so gallantly streaming?
> And the rockets' red glare, the bombs bursting in air,
> Gave proof through the night that our flag was still there.

Oh say, does that Star-Spangled Banner yet wave
O'er the land of the free and the home of the brave?

Just days before the Battle of Fort McHenry, United States naval forces in upstate New York repulsed a large British invasion out of Canada at the Battle of Lake Champlain (also known as the Battle of Plattsburgh).

Negotiations to end the conflict were already underway in Belgium. The Treaty of Ghent, signed by diplomats on Christmas Eve in 1814, called for an end to hostilities and a restoration of pre-war boundaries without addressing the principal issues that led to the taking up of arms. The British government approved the treaty before the end of the year, but the war continued until both nations ratified the document.

A major military campaign was fought in New Orleans in late December and early January. General Andrew Jackson, leading an American force composed of army regulars, state militias, Creoles, Choctaws, free blacks, and Jean Lafitte's band of pirates, fortified a line of defense against a larger British force. The redcoats lost 2,400 men before retreating; American troops suffered 300 casualties.

The United States Senate approved the Treaty of Ghent in February of 1815, bringing the war to a close. The War of 1812, sometimes called the second war of independence, created a strong feeling of national unity and pride even though it ended in a stalemate. America showed that it was willing and able to stand alone and defend itself against the most powerful nation in the world.

After that war ended, the U.S. asserted its military strength across the Atlantic. For centuries North Africa's Barbary states – Algeria, Tunisia, Tripoli (Libya), and Morocco – had supported pirates who terrorized the Mediterranean, raiding coastal towns, seizing foreign ships, and plundering their cargoes. The region's rulers exacted tribute from European nations and later the United States in return for unmolested transit, and they held their captives for ransom or sold them into slavery.

By the time the First Barbary War began in 1801, the United States had already paid $2 million. In 1805 a U.S. force consisting of eight Marines and hundreds of mostly Arab mercenaries marched 500 miles across the desert "to the shores of Tripoli." With U.S. naval support, they captured the port city of Derna and rescued 300 American sailors being held hostage. The war ended shortly thereafter.

But the piracy did not stop permanently, and a second war was waged. In 1815 the United States deployed a fleet of 10 Navy ships to the Mediterranean under the command of Stephen Decatur. He forced the Barbary states to return American prisoners and property, pay restitution, and cease their attacks on American shipping once and for all. The U.S. ended its tribute payments, and European nations followed suit.

* *"The Star-Spangled Banner" did not become the national anthem until 1931.*

† *walls of the fort*

24
WESTERN EXPANSION and INDUSTRIALIZATION

From the time of their first settlements on the East Coast, Americans kept pushing westward. For those who went, the adventure of settling new territory and the lure of low-cost or even free land outweighed the hardships and dangers of frontier life.

Western migration increased after the War of 1812. Roads and canals made it easier for people to travel and transport goods. The Cumberland Road, also called the National Road, was one of the first major improved highways in the country. It provided a land route between two important rivers, the Potomac and the Ohio, and continued westward into Illinois. The most significant man-made waterway was the Erie Canal, which stretched for 360 miles across New York State, from the Hudson River in the east to Lake Erie in the west. Initially four feet deep and 40 feet wide, the canal opened up another water route between the Great Lakes and the Atlantic Ocean. Horses, mules, or oxen hitched up to long ropes towed boats and barges up and down the canal.

Northern states experienced a rapid growth in industrialization: the use of machines to manufacture goods in larger quantities and often of higher quality than is possible with human labor alone. The first manufacturing plants were built along rivers, whose flowing waters provided power for the machines. With the advent of steam-powered engines, mechanized plants could operate virtually anywhere. Steam engines were also used to propel boats and trains at speeds that drastically reduced transportation times.

The South lagged far behind the North in the Industrial Revolution. Agriculture, the largest economic sector in both regions, was more dominant in the South, which enjoyed a longer growing season and had more large farms, or plantations.

SLAVERY

Slavery was an integral part of Southern life.* Its roots went back to colonial Jamestown. It was there in 1619 that a Dutch ship docked with 20 African captives on board.[†] John Rolfe paid for them, but it is uncertain whether their status in Virginia was that of slaves or indentured servants. The latter were obligated to work for a set period of time in exchange for passage, room and board, or other considerations that might include a tract of land. Such arrangements were usually voluntary, and the servant had legal rights. During the colonial period many Europeans came to America as indentured servants, but for Africans – involuntary, permanent, and inheritable servitude was the norm. Slaves were considered property.

The slaves came from African cultures with diverse social and political systems, long-distance trade networks, and urban communities with sophisticated architecture. Many different languages were spoken on the continent. Africans created complex works of art and musical forms. They were skilled metalworkers. Gold was a major export.

For centuries before Europeans entered the slave market, Africans had been enslaved and traded by other Africans and Arabs, but not in a systematic manner or for mass agricultural production, and their servitude was generally not perpetuated through generations.

European colonization of the Americas greatly increased the demand for labor, and Africa became the main supplier.[‡] Men, women, and children on the continent were abducted or otherwise acquired by other Africans and marched to the coast, where they became inventory for slave merchants to trade with their European counterparts. A slave might be thrown in with captives taken from different parts of Africa whose language and culture were foreign. Some slaves were branded with a hot iron to identify them as property of a certain owner.

The first major European player in the slave trade was Portugal. Its leading position was overtaken by the Dutch in the 17th century. By the end of the 18th century, England had become the foremost slave-trading nation.

Most slaves were brought to the Western Hemisphere in an economic cycle known as the Transatlantic Triangular Trade. European merchants sailed to Africa with guns, textiles, rum, and other manufactured goods, which were bartered for gold, ivory, and slaves. The captives were packed like cargo onto the ships for the next leg of the journey, the notorious Middle Passage across the Atlantic Ocean. In a few known cases, slaves who fell ill en route were pitched overboard to keep them from infecting other slaves and because the ship's insurance covered deaths due to drowning but not disease. Some slaves committed suicide by jumping into the sea rather than suffer the horrible conditions. Those who survived the crossing were traded for New World goods, which were loaded onto the ships for the return voyage to Europe to complete the triangle.[§]

As many as 12½ million Africans, a quarter of whom were children, were taken from their homelands for transport to the Western Hemisphere. Two million died in transit. The vast majority of slaves were taken to European colonies in South America and the Caribbean. The Portuguese colony of Brazil imported the most slaves by far, nearly five million, or 46 percent of the total. The number of slaves brought from Africa to the Thirteen Colonies (and later the United States) was small by comparison – around 390,000, or four percent of the total brought to the Americas.[¶]

Several of the nation's Founders, including George Washington, Thomas Jefferson, and James Madison, all Southern planters from Virginia, owned slaves. The Constitution addressed the slavery issue in three clauses. The first dealt with representation and taxation. Southern delegates to the Constitutional Convention wanted to exclude slaves for tax purposes but include them in the population count used to determine representation in the House of Representatives. The convention compromised by agreeing to include three-fifths of a state's slave population in the basis for both representation and direct taxes.

The second slavery clause in the Constitution prohibited any restriction on the importation of slaves before the year 1808. The third clause stipulated that slaves could not win their freedom by escaping across state lines and had to be returned to their masters if apprehended.

In 1793 Eli Whitney invented a machine that separated cotton fiber from its seed. His cotton gin greatly increased the amount of raw material that could be processed in a day and made the plant a highly lucrative crop. Cotton became "king" in the South, and the demand for slaves to work the fields grew.

The United States outlawed the importation of slaves in 1808, but the status of slaves already in the country did not change. The slave population more than tripled in the South over the next 50 years due to smuggling and high birth rates among existing slaves.[‖] Opposition to slavery on moral and religious grounds existed from colonial times, even as slavery became a common practice. That opposition dwindled in the South but grew more determined in the North.

---

* *Slavery was also practiced in Northern states but on a relatively small scale.*

† *The first African slaves transported to the Western Hemisphere were brought to the Spanish Caribbean nearly a century earlier, in 1526. By 1619 slavery was already well established on plantations throughout Spanish America and in the Portuguese colony of Brazil, where labor-intensive cane sugar was the main export.*

‡ *For the first three centuries after Columbus, the number of Africans brought to the New World far exceeded the number of Europeans who came, by a ratio of six to one. It was the largest forced migration in history.*

§ *There were variations to the triangle. For example, rum, fish, and agricultural goods from New England were shipped to Africa and exchanged for slaves, who were transported to the West Indies and traded for sugar, molasses, and coffee destined for New England. Some slaves were brought to the Thirteen Colonies (and later the United States) from the West Indies, where they had originally been brought from Africa.*

¶ *Distribution of African slaves brought to the Western Hemisphere:*

4.9 million	46%	*Portuguese Brazil*
2.3 million	22%	*British Caribbean*
1.3 million	12%	*Spanish America*
1.1 million	11%	*French Caribbean*
440,000	4%	*Dutch Caribbean*
390,000	4%	*Thirteen Colonies / United States*
110,000	1%	*Danish Caribbean*

‖ *The Southern slave population in 1810 was 1.2 million. By 1860 the number had risen to four million. In South Carolina and Mississippi, slaves outnumbered whites.*

26
MISSOURI COMPROMISE and the MONROE DOCTRINE

As the population grew in the territories west of the original 13 states, new states were formed, some in the North and some in the South. By the year 1819 there were 22 states in the country. Slavery was prohibited or in the process of being abolished in the 11 Northern states:

New Hampshire	Connecticut	New Jersey	Indiana
Vermont	Rhode Island	Pennsylvania	Illinois
Massachusetts	New York	Ohio	

Slavery was legal in the 11 Southern states:

Delaware	North Carolina	Kentucky	Louisiana
Maryland	South Carolina	Tennessee	Mississippi
Virginia	Georgia	Alabama	

With the same number of Northern free states and Southern slave states, each side was equally represented in the U.S. Senate.

A conflict arose when Missouri applied for statehood. Slavery was already established in the territory. Allowing Missouri to become a state would tip the balance in the Senate in favor of slave states. In 1820 Congress reached an agreement known as the Missouri Compromise. Maine, which was part of Massachusetts, would be admitted as a free state to balance Missouri's admission as a slave state. The legislation banned slavery in the rest of the Louisiana Territory north of the latitude line corresponding to Missouri's southern border.*

The Missouri Compromise did not end the debate. Continued Northern opposition to slavery threatened the economy and social order of the South. John Adams and Thomas Jefferson, still alive in 1820, worried that the brewing conflict would erupt into a civil war and split the nation they helped found.

In foreign affairs, an independence movement was underway in Latin America. Colombia separated from Spain in 1810. Over the next 12 years, Mexico and most of the other Spanish colonies declared independence as well. In 1822 Brazil broke away from Portugal. To the north, Russia laid claim to territory in the Pacific Northwest. These developments raised concerns that European nations might try to increase their influence in the Americas. It was in this context that President James Monroe made a bold declaration of U.S. foreign policy in 1823. The Monroe Doctrine asserted that:

- Neither American continent was to be considered for future colonization by any European powers.

- Any attempt by European powers to exert control, extend their political system, or interfere with nations in the Western Hemisphere would be considered dangerous to the peace and safety of the U.S.

- The United States would not interfere in the internal affairs of European nations or with their existing colonies in the Americas.

* *The Missouri Compromise Line should not be confused with the Mason-Dixon Line, established in colonial times to settle a border dispute between Pennsylvania and Maryland. The Mason-Dixon Line came to symbolize the cultural boundary between the North and the South.*

27
JACKSONIAN DEMOCRACY and TARIFFS

The Constitution left it up to the states to determine who was eligible to vote in elections. Most states required voters to be taxpayers or landowners. The lifting of those restrictions beginning in 1807 led to a widening of political participation in the country and paved the way for Andrew Jackson's presidency (1829-37).

Born in humble circumstances in the backwoods of the Carolinas without the advantages of earlier presidents, Jackson had a natural appeal to the common man. He fought in the Revolutionary War as a youth, moved to Tennessee in his early twenties to practice law, represented the state in the U.S. Congress, and served on the Tennessee Supreme Court before becoming a hero in the War of 1812. In 1828 he was elected the seventh president of the United States and was the first from an interior state. "Jacksonian democracy" manifested itself in political rallies and parades, partisan newspapers, higher voter turnout, and greater party loyalty.

President Jackson, a Democrat, had to confront the growing sectionalism in the country. Slavery was not the only issue dividing the North and the South; sharp disagreements arose over tariffs.

A tariff is a tax on imported goods. Also called duties, tariffs are a source of revenue for the federal government* and a means of protecting domestic producers from foreign competition.

To illustrate how tariffs work, assume that American stores sell only two kinds of chairs, those imported from France that sell for $10 apiece and those made in America that sell for $12. Most consumers would buy the cheaper French chair. With more of their chairs being sold, French chair manufacturers make more money, build more factories, and hire more French workers.

When the federal government adds a $5 tariff to French chairs, most U.S. consumers would buy the now-cheaper American chair.[†] With more of their product being sold, American chair manufacturers make more money, build more factories, and hire more American workers. Some people would continue to buy French chairs, even at the higher price, if they had a strong preference for the foreign product or if domestic producers could not make enough chairs to satisfy demand. The tariffs, which are collected from American importers, flow into the U.S. treasury.

French Chair		American Chair
$10	price before tariff	$12
+ $ 5	American tariff on French chairs	n/a
$15	price after tariff	$12

Tariffs can be levied on raw materials and farm products as well as manufactured goods.

U.S. imports decreased sharply during the Napoleonic Wars in Europe and the War of 1812. The difficulty in procuring manufactured goods from abroad highlighted the need for an American industrial base both as a matter of national security and to balance an economy dominated by agriculture and shipping. Manufacturing was growing in the Northern states, but European industry was more established, especially in Great Britain, and could produce goods more efficiently and cheaply. The United States raised tariffs in 1816, 1824, and 1828 to protect domestic manufacturers from lower-priced imports and help infant American industries develop a home market. The rates of the 1828 tariff were so exorbitant that Southerners called it the "Tariff of Abominations."

When the federal government laid a tariff on a product, all U.S. consumers, those in the North and the South, who were accustomed to buying cheaper imports of that product, had to pay more. The higher prices were more palatable to Northerners because of the benefits tariffs brought to their region. Tariffs resulted in increased sales for Northern manufacturers and more jobs for Northern workers. Since their products were made primarily for the domestic market, Northerners did not have to worry about the effect American tariffs had overseas.

For Southerners there was no silver lining to the higher prices they had to pay for manufactured goods. The region had relatively few manufacturing businesses and workers that could benefit from tariff protection. Moreover, Southerners relied heavily on sales of their agricultural products abroad. Retaliatory tariffs by foreign countries could close off those lucrative markets. Cotton alone accounted for half of all U.S. exports.

Southerners questioned the constitutionality of the tariffs because they gave preference to certain states. Tariffs were also viewed as a backdoor attack on slavery.

The federal government lowered tariff rates in 1832 but not enough to placate South Carolina. The state legislature passed an ordinance that nullified the tariffs of 1828 and 1832, declared them unconstitutional, forbade the collection of duties in the state, and threatened secession from the United States if attempts were made to force their compliance. By assuming a right to secede and a right to unilaterally repeal federal law, South Carolina challenged the supremacy of the national government and the Constitution.

To show that he fully intended to enforce the tariff laws of the country, President Jackson, though a Southerner and a slaveholder, sent naval ships and a contingent of soldiers to reinforce two forts in

Charleston Harbor. A violent confrontation between federal troops and the state militia was averted when the U.S. Congress passed a bill in 1833 that reduced tariffs even further, and South Carolina rescinded its nullification ordinance.

From 1789 to 1909, tariffs were the largest source of federal revenue in all but 12 years.

† *A tariff's effect on price can be mitigated by manufacturers, wholesalers, and retailers accepting lower profit margins.*

28
TRAIL of TEARS,
MANIFEST DESTINY, and GOLD

In 1830 President Jackson signed the Indian Removal Act into law. The legislation authorized him to grant federal territory west of the Mississippi River to tribes who relinquished their ancestral lands. The government promised to assist with the relocation and provide physical protection after tribes arrived at their assigned destinations, most of which were in present-day Oklahoma. The exodus of Native Americans (especially the Cherokee) from the Southern states is remembered as the "Trail of Tears." Their journey was marked by cruelty and privation.

In the 1820s American settlers pushed westward into Texas, which at the time was part of Mexico. Led by Stephen Austin, they were welcomed at first, but the huge influx that followed alarmed the Mexican government. When Mexico tried to reassert control over the territory, the settlers fought back.

The most famous battle in that struggle took place in 1836 at the Alamo, a fort in San Antonio that was originally a Spanish mission. Two hundred men, Texas settlers and volunteers from the U.S., were determined to hold the fort. The garrison included American folk heroes Davy Crockett and Jim Bowie. A Mexican army of 3,000 commanded by General Santa Anna laid siege to the Alamo for 13 days before finally overwhelming and killing the defenders.

The remaining Texas forces, led by Sam Houston, rallied and defeated Santa Anna the following month. Texans had already declared their independence and formed a separate nation: the Republic of Texas. In 1845 Texas joined the U.S. as the 28th state.

The United States declared war on Mexico in 1846 after Mexicans attacked American troops in a disputed area along the Rio Grande River. U.S. forces captured the capital of Mexico City the following year and occupied the National Palace, or "the halls of Montezuma."

The Mexican War ended in 1848 with ratification of the Treaty of Guadalupe Hidalgo. The U.S. acquired present-day California, Nevada, Utah, most of Arizona, and parts of New Mexico, Colorado, and Wyoming. For Mexico, it was a loss of 40 percent of its territory. In return, the U.S. agreed to pay Mexico $15 million and satisfy up to $3.25 million in claims filed by Americans against the Mexican government. The 75,000 Mexicans living in what was now U.S. territory would become American citizens by default after one year if they did not exercise their option to retain Mexican citizenship. Most became U.S. citizens.

Before the war ended, members of the Church of Jesus Christ of Latter-day Saints, commonly known as Mormons, entered the Salt Lake Valley after being driven out of Illinois by mobs. Under the leadership of Brigham Young, Mormons settled Utah and other parts of the West.

In the Northwest, the United States and Great Britain resolved a disagreement over the Oregon Territory without war. A treaty in 1846 made the present-day states of Oregon, Washington, Idaho, and parts of Montana and Wyoming undisputed U.S. territory.

The Oregon Territory, the Mexican Cession, and Texas all became part of the United States during James K. Polk's presidency (1845-49). This additional 770 million acres, more land than was acquired with the Louisiana Purchase, extended the country's western boundary to the Pacific Ocean. Americans believed the expansion across the continent was "Manifest Destiny," or obvious and inevitable.*

In 1848 gold was discovered near Sacramento, California, at a sawmill belonging to John Sutter. The news spread quickly and spawned a gold rush. Eighty thousand "Forty-niners" streamed into California the following year. Discoveries of gold and silver in Nevada, Colorado, and elsewhere also drew thousands of prospectors westward.

During this same period, European and Asian immigrants came to America in large numbers to seek greater economic opportunity and escape political unrest. A million immigrants came from Ireland alone because of a potato famine there.

---

* In 1854 the U.S. acquired 19 million additional acres from Mexico. The Gadsden Purchase, named for U.S. diplomat James Gadsden who negotiated the deal, expanded the southern borders of Arizona and New Mexico at a cost of $10 million.

ABOLITION

Abolitionists wanted to bring an end to slavery throughout the U.S., and some were willing to violate fugitive slave laws. They organized the Underground Railroad, a network of people who hid escaped slaves and secretly transported them to free states and Canada instead of returning them to their masters, as required by law. Harriet Tubman, an escaped slave herself, is called "the Moses of her people" for leading hundreds to freedom.

The most prominent abolitionist was Frederick Douglass, also an escaped slave. The success of his autobiography in America and Europe and his eloquent and moving speeches helped dispel the notion that blacks were inherently intellectually inferior. While he was lecturing in England, his friends paid off his former master, making Douglass legally free.*

In 1852 Harriet Beecher Stowe published her novel, *Uncle Tom's Cabin.* Inspired by fugitive slave laws, it portrayed the evils of slavery in a dramatic manner and had a significant impact on public opinion in the North.

The Kansas-Nebraska Act, signed by President Franklin Pierce in 1854, carved two new territories out of the Louisiana Territory. To appease pro-slavery factions, a "popular sovereignty" provision in the legislation left it up to the electorate in each territory to decide whether or not slavery would be allowed. Both of the new territories were north of Missouri's southern border and supposedly off-limits to slavery, according to the Missouri Compromise of 1820. The Kansas-Nebraska Act, in effect, nullified the earlier law. This angered Northerners and led to the formation of a new political party: the Republican Party.

Nebraska was too far north to attract slaveholders, but Kansas became a battleground. The supporters and the opponents of slavery came into the territory hoping to affect the outcome of the vote. Deadly clashes between the two groups earned the territory the nickname "Bleeding Kansas" before it was admitted to the Union as a free state.

The Supreme Court handed down a ruling known as the Dred Scott decision in 1857. Dred Scott, a slave owned by a Missouri surgeon, had lived for a time with his master in the Wisconsin Territory and in the state of Illinois. Scott filed suit on the grounds that residing even temporarily where slavery was illegal had made him a free man. The Supreme Court disagreed. In the majority opinion issued by the court, the justices held that slaves were property with no constitutional rights, and the Missouri Compromise was unconstitutional and had always been null and void. Southerners hailed the decision. Northerners were outraged.

John Brown, a radical abolitionist, believed he was an instrument of God to help bring an end to slavery. In 1859 he and several accomplices failed in their attempt to seize the federal arsenal at Harpers Ferry in western Virginia. They had planned to lead slaves in an armed uprising. Brown and six others were hanged after being convicted of murder, treason, and conspiring to produce an insurrection. Northern abolitionists regarded him as a martyr. In the South, Harpers Ferry stoked long-standing fears of a slave revolt.[†]

---

* *By 1860 there were half a million free blacks in the U.S., with slightly more in the South than in the North. They or their ancestors had become free in a variety of ways, such as satisfying their terms of indenture or simply being set free by their masters. Some had migrated as free people from other lands. Many blacks in Louisiana were free when the United States purchased the territory from France in 1803. Thousands of free blacks in the South were slave owners.*

[†] *In 1831 Nat Turner, a slave on a Virginia plantation, led a revolt that left 55 whites, mostly women and children, dead. A militia killed a number of innocent slaves along with some of the insurgents before order was restored. Turner and 16 followers were hanged.*

30
ABRAHAM LINCOLN,
SECESSION, and CIVIL WAR

Tensions between the North and the South reached a critical stage in 1860 when the Republican Party's candidate, Abraham Lincoln of Illinois, was elected the 16th president of the United States. Lincoln opposed slavery and its expansion into the western territories but was willing to let it continue where it already existed. That position was unacceptable to most Southerners although only a quarter of households in the South were slaveholders. Southerners believed slavery was essential to their economy and way of life. Limiting its expansion was considered a threat.

Even before Lincoln was sworn in, Southern states began breaking away from the United States. South Carolina was first. Mississippi, Florida,* Alabama, Georgia, Louisiana, and Texas soon followed. They formed a separate nation known as the Confederate States of America and chose Jefferson Davis of Mississippi as their president.[†]

President Lincoln pleaded for reconciliation in his inaugural address.

> We are not enemies, but friends. We must not be enemies. Though passion may have strained, it must not break our bonds of affection. The mystic chords of memory, stretching from every battlefield and patriot grave, to every living heart and hearthstone, all over this broad land, will yet swell the chorus of the Union, when again touched, as they surely will be, by the better angels of our nature.

Southerners were unmoved. States that seceded took possession of federal property within their borders. Fort Sumter, however, situated on a small man-made island at the entrance to the harbor in Charleston, South Carolina, remained in federal hands. By April 1861, provisions at the fort were running low. President Lincoln notified South Carolina that he was sending ships to resupply the fort. On the morning of April 12, before the ships arrived, rebels began bombarding the fort, igniting a civil war in America. The garrison of 80 federal troops defending Fort Sumter surrendered the next day.

After the fall of Fort Sumter, four more Southern states seceded: Virginia, Arkansas, Tennessee, and North Carolina. The Confederacy established its capital in Richmond, Virginia – only 100 miles south of Washington, D.C.

The border slave states of Missouri, Kentucky, Maryland, and Delaware did not join the Confederacy. Also, the northwestern counties of Virginia refused to follow the decision of their state legislature to secede. That region was later admitted to the U.S. as the state of West Virginia. While these border states remained in the Union, they were, nevertheless, home to many Confederate sympathizers and contributed soldiers to both armies.

The two sides in the Civil War were differentiated as follows:

Section of the Country	North	South (Dixie)
Government	United States of America / USA / Union	Confederate States of America / CSA / Confederacy
President	Abraham Lincoln	Jefferson Davis
Soldier/Citizen	Yankee	Rebel
Color of Uniform	Blue	Gray

From the outset, the Union had tremendous advantages. It had a population of more than 22 million people in 23 states and the federal territories. The population in the 11 states of the Confederacy was less than nine million, 3½ million (40 percent) of whom were slaves. The North had more factories to produce weapons and other military supplies. It had better roads and more steamboats, barges, and railroads. The Union had an established navy. The Confederacy, for the most part, had to build its navy from scratch.

The political philosophy of the Confederate states worked against them. Their belief in the primacy of states' rights led them to resist the central organization necessary to win a war.

The South was not without advantages, though. In the beginning of the war, the Confederacy had more aggressive military leaders and better horsemen. To win, it had only to maintain defensive positions on familiar terrain. For the North to win, it would have to take the offensive, invade the South, and force Confederate states back into the Union, which would require more resources and longer supply lines. Despite the fact that Europe had abolished slavery decades earlier, Southerners expected European nations, consumers of their agricultural goods, to come to their aid and pressure the Union to recognize the Confederacy. The antebellum South produced two-thirds of the world's raw cotton and 80 percent of the cotton used by Britain's textile industry. All of these factors gave Southerners confidence they could win their independence.

* *Spain was forced to cede Florida to the British in 1763 but reacquired the territory after the Revolutionary War. The United States acquired Florida in 1819 through a treaty with Spain in which the U.S. renounced any territorial rights to Texas and agreed to pay up to $5 million in legal claims brought by American citizens against Spain. In 1845 the U.S. admitted Florida as the 27th state.*

† *Jefferson Davis had been a U.S. senator and was secretary of war in the Pierce administration. In the latter capacity he strengthened the military that the Confederacy would eventually have to fight.*

31
ULYSSES S. GRANT, ROBERT E. LEE,
and EMANCIPATION

After fighting broke out, President Lincoln ordered a naval blockade of Confederate ports. Enforcing a barrier across 3,000 miles of Southern coastline was impossible at first. Blockade runners were able to easily slip past the Union navy. But as more and more coastal territory would come under Union control over the course of the war, the blockade would help strangle the Confederacy by choking off its exports and cutting off supplies coming in by sea.

The first major contest between Union and Confederate armies took place in Virginia at the Battle of Bull Run (also known as the Battle of Manassas), only 30 miles west of Washington, D.C. It was fought in 1861, a few months after the fall of Fort Sumter. Each side began the battle with around 30,000 men. Hundreds of citizens came out from Washington to be close to the spectacle. They were shocked by the outcome. Before the day was over, spectators and defeated Union soldiers were fleeing back to the safety of the U.S. capital.

The first key battles of 1862 were fought in Tennessee. Union General Ulysses S. Grant captured 12,000 Confederate soldiers when he took Fort Donelson. Two months later a Confederate attack caught him unprepared at the Battle of Shiloh, but he rallied his troops and, with reinforcements, beat back the Rebels, though at a great cost.

The Confederacy suffered a calamity when a Union naval squadron under the command of David Farragut captured New Orleans and closed off the mouth of the Mississippi River, one of the South's main supply routes. The Rebels deployed a new kind of weapon, the ironclad, in their unsuccessful defense of the city. These warships, developed by both Union and Confederate navies, were covered with metal plates to deflect bullets and cannon shells.

By the middle of 1862 the Union controlled western Tennessee and much of the lower Mississippi River.

It was a different story in the East. After winning a second battle at Bull Run, the Rebels captured the federal arsenal at Harpers Ferry along with 13,000 Union troops. Confederate General Robert E. Lee then led his army 10 miles farther north, across the Potomac River and into western Maryland. At the Battle of Antietam (also known as the Battle of Sharpsburg), Lee fought the Union army to a draw despite being outnumbered two to one and despite having had his battle plans carelessly fall into Union hands. The combined Union and Confederate casualties − 3,600 dead and 17,000 wounded − made Antietam the bloodiest one-day battle of the war. Later that year, the Confederacy scored a victory at Fredericksburg in Virginia.

In September of 1862, less than a week after Antietam, President Lincoln issued an executive order giving the Confederate states 100 days to end their rebellion and retain a legal right to practice slavery. None of the states accepted the offer.

The day the ultimatum expired, January 1, 1863, Lincoln issued a follow-up executive order known as the Emancipation Proclamation.

It made slaves legally free, but only in areas of the South still controlled by the Rebels. Ironically, the proclamation did not apply to slaves in parts of the Confederacy already under Union control, nor did it apply to slaves in the border states that had remained loyal to the Union. Nevertheless, the Emancipation Proclamation marked the first time President Lincoln formally made the abolition of slavery a principal aim of the war. The order also authorized the enlistment of freed slaves for military service. Nearly 180,000 blacks would serve in the U.S. Army during the war, and another 19,000 joined the Navy.

32
GETTYSBURG

In May 1863 a Confederate army led by Robert E. Lee defeated a larger Union army at Chancellorsville, Virginia. During the battle Lee's reliable officer, Thomas "Stonewall" Jackson, was returning to the Confederate lines at night when he was shot by a North Carolina regiment that mistook him and his staff for Yankees. Jackson was thought to be recovering following the amputation of his left arm, but he contracted pneumonia and died eight days after being shot. He had earned his nickname by being fearless and unyielding in battle.

Jackson's death was a blow to General Lee and the Confederacy, but, encouraged by the victory at Chancellorsville, Lee led his troops into the North. He hoped to inflict such heavy losses on the Union army that President Lincoln would be pressured to sue for peace, since the high number of casualties was weakening public support for the war.

The two armies clashed at the small Pennsylvania town of Gettysburg. Seventy-five thousand Confederates faced 95,000 Union troops in a three-day engagement that became the most well-known battle of the war and produced the most casualties.

It began on July 1, 1863. After two days the battle had been fought to a draw. On July 3, the Union and Confederate armies held opposite ridges with an open field between them. General Lee ordered a daring assault that became known as Pickett's Charge, General George Pickett being one of the Southern commanders directing the attack. As Rebel soldiers poured onto the field, they were slaughtered by Union cannon and rifle fire. Those who made it across fought their way up the opposing ridge, but the Union lines held, and the Rebels had to pull back. Confederate casualties were approximately 50 percent. After bracing for a Union counterattack that never came, Lee's army retreated in a driving rain.

The number of Union and Confederate soldiers killed in action at Gettysburg was around 7,500. The number of wounded or missing exceeded 43,000 by some estimates. Although the Union victory was a turning point, it did not bring a quick end to the war. Fighting continued for two more years, with almost as many casualties after the battle as before.

President Lincoln attended the dedication of a Union cemetery at Gettysburg a few months after the battle. The first speaker addressed the crowd for two hours. Lincoln followed. His Gettysburg Address lasted only a couple of minutes. He said:

> Four score and seven years ago* our fathers brought forth on this continent a new nation, conceived in liberty, and dedicated to the proposition that all men are created equal.
>
> Now we are engaged in a great civil war testing whether that nation, or any nation so conceived and so dedicated, can long endure. We are met on a great battlefield of that war. We have come to dedicate a portion of that field as a final resting place for those who here gave their lives that that nation might live. It is altogether fitting and proper that we should do this.
>
> But, in a larger sense, we can not dedicate – we can not consecrate – we can not hallow – this ground. The brave men, living and dead, who struggled here, have consecrated it, far above our poor power to add or detract. The world will little note, nor long remember what we say here, but it can never forget what they did here. It is for us the living, rather, to be dedicated here to the unfinished work which they who fought here have thus far so nobly advanced. It is rather for us to be here dedicated to the great task remaining before us – that from these honored dead we take increased devotion to that cause for which they gave the last full measure of devotion – that we here highly resolve that these dead shall not have died in vain – that this nation, under God, shall have a new birth of freedom – and that government of the people, by the people, for the people, shall not perish from the earth.

* *"Score" is another word for twenty. Four times twenty plus seven equals 87. The year referenced by Lincoln, 87 years prior to 1863, was 1776, the year America declared independence.*

33

MARCH TO THE SEA,
APPOMATTOX, and FORD'S THEATER

On July 4, 1863, the day after the Battle of Gettysburg ended and a thousand miles away, 29,000 Confederate soldiers defending the heavily fortified city of Vicksburg, Mississippi, surrendered after a six-week siege. The victory gave the Union control of the entire Mississippi River and split the Confederacy in two.

Later that year, the Rebels beat Union troops at the Battle of Chickamauga in northern Georgia but were unable to retake Chattanooga, Tennessee, just 10 miles to the north. The Union's numerical and industrial superiority were becoming more apparent. The Confederacy's only hope was to exhaust the North's will to fight.

In September 1864 Union troops commanded by William Tecumseh Sherman captured the Confederate stronghold of Atlanta, Georgia. General Sherman then began his "March to the Sea" to the port city of Savannah. Advancing in a wide swath, his men not only fought Confederate soldiers and destroyed railroads and bridges, they also laid waste to homes, barns, crops, and other private property in the state. Southerners resented the wanton destruction, but Sherman believed the war would end sooner if Confederate citizens as well as soldiers were convinced that the price for continuing the fight was too high.

In Virginia a series of battles known as the Wilderness Campaign was fought in May and June of 1864. Pitted against each other were the two main armies in the East: the Army of the Potomac led by Ulysses S. Grant and the Army of Northern Virginia led by Robert E. Lee. Both sides won individual battles and inflicted enormous casualties, but the overall campaign was a strategic victory for the Union. It forced Lee into a defensive position to protect the Confederate capital of Richmond and the neighboring city of Petersburg. After a 10-month siege, both cities fell in early April of 1865.

General Lee escaped with his army but soon found himself hemmed in and vastly outnumbered by Union forces. Concluding that it was pointless to continue, he surrendered to General Grant on April 9 at Appomattox, Virginia. As the news spread, Confederate units in other parts of the South also gave up. The Civil War was finally over.

The war took the lives of an estimated 620,000 Union and Confederate troops. As costly as the battles were, disease accounted for a majority of those deaths. Of the 470,000 soldiers who survived their wounds, many were permanently maimed. Parts of the South lay in ruins. But the war brought an end to slavery for four million blacks. It reestablished the preeminence of national interests over states' rights, settled the question of whether a state had the right to secede, and confirmed the supremacy of the Constitution and federal law over contradictory state law.

Lincoln formulated a lenient plan to restore the Confederate states to their place in the Union. The Constitution did not address the issue. The process, known as Reconstruction, was already underway in parts of Louisiana, Tennessee, Arkansas, and Virginia before the war ended. The Freedmen's Bureau had been created to assist former slaves with food, housing, medical care, employment, education, and legal matters. The agency also helped reunite family members. Congress had passed the 13th Amendment to abolish slavery constitutionally and formally free those slaves not freed by the Emancipation Proclamation.

Less than a week after Appomattox, as President Lincoln was beginning his second term and shifting his focus to postwar issues, he and his wife invited another couple to accompany them to a play at Ford's Theater, five blocks from the White House. While Lincoln and his party watched the comedy from the presidential box, John Wilkes Booth, a 26-year-old actor not involved in the performance, crept up behind the president and shot him. Booth, a Southern sympathizer, leapt down onto the stage and broke his leg but managed to escape.

President Lincoln's wound was fatal, and he died the next morning, never regaining consciousness.* Union soldiers killed Booth 12 days later, after finding him hiding in a barn 70 miles from Washington, D.C. Four others implicated in the assassination were hanged after their convictions by a military tribunal. In accordance with the Constitution, Vice-President Andrew Johnson, a former slaveholder from Tennessee, assumed the presidency upon Lincoln's death.

* Lincoln was the first president to be assassinated, but two of his predecessors also died in office. William Henry Harrison, the 9th president, died of enteric fever one month after his inauguration in 1841. Zachary Taylor, the 12th president, succumbed to severe gastroenteritis in 1850, 16 months into his term.

34
RECONSTRUCTION and IMPEACHMENT

President Johnson's Reconstruction plan, like Lincoln's, was lenient and conciliatory. Property confiscated from Southerners during the war was returned.* Most Southerners who pledged allegiance to the

United States and took an oath to accept the abolition of slavery were granted amnesty and had their rights as citizens restored, but large property holders and high-ranking leaders in the Confederate military and government could be pardoned only by the president.[†]

In the former Confederate states that had not already begun Reconstruction under Lincoln, President Johnson appointed civilian provisional governors to provide oversight of his plan. To reestablish loyal government, special elections were held in the South to select delegates to state conventions. The conventions were expected to ratify the 13th Amendment which abolished slavery, renounce any right to secession, cancel all war debts owed to their state and the Confederacy, and amend or rewrite their state constitutions with those provisions. Elections were then held for state and federal offices.

By December 1865, eight months after the end of the war, new governments were functioning in the former Confederate states and President Johnson, satisfied with their progress, was ready to reinstate them into the Union.

Congress objected for a number of reasons. Confederate leaders had been elected to office. Former slaves had not been given the right to vote, and Black Codes had been enacted to keep them under a form of slavery. Blacks could be arrested and fined for not having a job, then be forced to work to pay the fine. Some of the codes placed constraints on when and where they could travel, limited employment to agriculture or domestic service, imposed restrictions on land ownership,[‡] and made owning a gun, preaching without a license, and fishing illegal. Former slaves were targets of violence, including lynching. Some of the perpetrators acted openly; others hid behind the cloak of secret societies such as the Ku Klux Klan (KKK).

Asserting authority over the process, Congress implemented its own Reconstruction plan. The congressional leadership refused to seat representatives and senators elected from the South under the president's plan. Congress passed the 14th Amendment to the Constitution that, upon ratification:

- made citizens of all persons born or naturalized in the U.S., which included former slaves

- prohibited states from denying equal protection of the laws or depriving citizens of their personal liberties without due process of law

- voided all debts incurred to aid the rebellion

- voided all claims for losses resulting from emancipation

- authorized the reduction of a state's representation in the House of Representatives in proportion to that state's denial of voting rights to adult males

- prohibited former public officials from holding office in the government or the military at the state or federal level if they had supported the rebellion after taking an oath to uphold the Constitution (Congress could make individual exceptions)

Congress divided the South into five military districts, each under the control of a Union general with broad authority to oversee the congressional Reconstruction plan. Federal troops were deployed to provide enforcement if necessary. To reassume its place in the Union, a state was expected to:

- ratify the 14th Amendment

- register all adult males to vote and safeguard their voting rights

- elect delegates to a state convention to rewrite their state constitution again and make it acceptable to Congress

Congress remained at odds with President Johnson and in 1868 tried to oust him. The Constitution grants Congress that authority if a president is found guilty of "treason, bribery, or other high crimes and misdemeanors."

The process begins in the House of Representatives. A resolution is drafted specifying the alleged misconduct in one or more articles of impeachment. After debating the resolution, the House votes on each article or on the resolution as a whole. If even one of the articles passes by a simple majority, the president is impeached. The resolution is then sent to the Senate, where a two-thirds vote is required to find the president guilty and remove him from office.

The House of Representatives impeached Andrew Johnson, but the Senate fell one vote short of convicting him, and he continued as president.

A couple of months later, seven of the eleven Confederate states were readmitted to the Union after complying with the Reconstruction plan of Congress.

On Christmas Day in 1868, President Johnson issued a blanket pardon to everyone who had participated in the Confederate rebellion.

Ulysses S. Grant succeeded Johnson as president the following year. In 1870 the remaining former Confederate states – Virginia, Mississippi, Texas, and Georgia – were readmitted to the Union after meeting an additional requirement to ratify the 15th Amendment, which made it illegal to deny voting rights based on race.

All the Southern states were once again fully participating in the national government. Blacks were elected to local offices, state legislatures, and the U.S. Congress for the first time in history. Reconstruction ended in 1877 when the last federal troops stationed in the South withdrew.

The Civil War was one of the greatest crises in American history, but the fundamental structure of the government established by the Framers survived, and the country rebounded.

---

* *After Robert E. Lee and his family fled south at the beginning of the war, Union soldiers occupied his estate, Arlington, just across the Potomac River from Washington, D.C. The land was used to bury Union war dead and as a settlement for former slaves. Following a long legal battle eventually decided by the Supreme Court, the federal government purchased the property from the family for $150,000 in 1883, and it remained a national cemetery.*

† *Andrew Johnson granted 13,500 individual pardons during his presidency.*

‡ *Land ownership among former slaves remained low even after Black Codes were outlawed. By the turn of the century, 35 years after the Civil War ended, only 25 percent of Southern blacks owned at least part of the land they farmed, compared to 63 percent of white farmers.*

35
BIG BUSINESS

The economic and industrial strength of the U.S. increased dramatically after the Civil War, owing to several factors:

- Deposits of oil, natural gas, coal, metal ore, and other valuable raw materials were discovered.

- Shrewd businessmen formed companies that produced and distributed goods and services efficiently.

- A burst of creativity brought a flood of inventions.

- A large and growing number of workers were available, millions of whom had immigrated from Europe and Asia.

- Electricity and the internal combustion engine provided new means of generating power.

Three industries – railroads, steel, and oil – had an enormous impact on postwar growth.

Railroads

Thirty thousand miles of railroad track had already been laid in the U.S. by the year 1860. Railroad companies added 163,000 more miles over the next four decades. Federal, state, and local governments subsidized some of the construction with loans and land grants totaling 131 million acres, an area roughly the size of Utah and New Mexico.

One of the leading railroad barons of the period was Cornelius Vanderbilt. George Pullman made sleeping cars popular. Dining and socializing cars were also put into service.

Of all the railroad projects undertaken in the 19th century, none was more exciting or daunting than the first transcontinental railroad. Rail lines originating in the East extended only halfway across the country. The effort to bridge the 1,700-mile gap to the Pacific Coast began in 1863 during the Civil War. One company started laying track in Nebraska heading westward; another company started in California heading eastward.

The pace intensified after the war, and in 1869 the goal was achieved when the two lines met at Promontory Summit in Utah Territory. To mark the event, railroad executives ceremonially fastened the last segment of track into place using a commemorative golden spike. With the nation now connected by rail from the Atlantic Ocean to the Pacific, coast-to-coast travel was reduced from months to less than a week.

Reliable arrival and departure times were a necessity, but scheduling was difficult without a time standard throughout the country. Acting on their own, railroad companies implemented a plan, later adopted by the federal government, that divided the continental United States into four time zones exactly one hour apart. The transition took place on Sunday, November 18, 1883. As standard-time noon came to each of the zones in the country – Eastern, Central, Mountain, and Pacific – local clocks all across the zone were reset. It is remembered as "the day of two noons."

Steel

New methods for refining iron ore that were implemented after the Civil War made it feasible to mass produce steel, a stronger and more durable metal than iron. Pennsylvania led the nation in steel production, and Pittsburgh was the center of the industry. The state's foundries had forged 80 percent of the iron used by the Union military. Iron ore was mined in many parts of the country, but the richest deposits of high-quality ore were found in the Great Lakes region, particularly in northern Minnesota's Mesabi Range.

The leading figure in steel production and vertical integration in business was Andrew Carnegie. He owned not only the factories that manufactured steel, but also the mines where the ore was excavated and the ships and railroads used to transport his raw materials and finished goods.

Oil

Crude oil that oozed to the surface or seeped into brine or water wells had long been considered a nuisance or, at best, a byproduct. When oil's useful properties were fully recognized, entrepreneurs dug wells specifically to extract the "black gold." Edwin Drake drilled the first commercial oil well in 1858 in Pennsylvania. Other businessmen built refineries to turn the raw material into kerosene for lamps, gasoline for engines, and lubricants to make machines run smoothly.

In 1870 John D. Rockefeller founded the Standard Oil Company. By absorbing competing companies (horizontal integration) through buyouts or selling below cost if necessary to drive them out of business, he gained control of 90 percent of the petroleum refining capacity in the United States and became the richest person in the world and America's first billionaire.

Other Industries

Textile manufacturing was at the forefront of American industrialization going back to the 1700s. New England continued its dominance for decades after the Civil War, accounting for 76 percent of all U.S. spindles in 1890.* Powered sewing machines, paper patterns, and the standardization of clothing sizes led to mass production of ready-made clothing.

Charles Pillsbury developed methods for mass producing high-quality flour. By the early 1900s his mills were the largest such enterprise in the world.

Philip Armour and Gustavus Swift were leaders in meat packing. The invention of the refrigerated railroad car accelerated the growth of the industry.

Improvements to fertilizers, insecticides, plows, reapers, seed planters, and poultry incubators increased agricultural output.

Business owners needed to borrow money to start and expand large-scale operations. Many turned to J.P. Morgan, the foremost financier of the period.

---

* *The South would eclipse New England as the dominant textile manufacturing region by 1930.*

36

INVENTION, ENTREPRENEURS, and PHILANTHROPY

Thomas Edison is considered one of the greatest inventors of all time. In 1877 he built the phonograph to record and play back sound. To see if it worked, he recited the children's poem, "Mary Had a Little Lamb," and was surprised to hear his voice reproduced on the first attempt. The following year he filed a patent for an electric light bulb, an invention that brought him universal fame. Edison obtained patents on more than a thousand other inventions, including electric generators, various types of batteries, and motion picture cameras and projectors.

Alexander Graham Bell was trying to help the hearing-impaired when he came up with the idea for the telephone. In 1876 he was ready to test his invention, which had two main components. He placed the receiver in one room of his laboratory and the transmitter in another and connected the two by wire. With his assistant in the other room, Bell spoke into the transmitter, "Mr. Watson, come here. I want to see you." The assistant heard Bell's voice coming through the receiver and quickly responded. The telephone would eventually replace the telegraph, a device developed by Samuel B. Morse that sent and received coded electrical pulses over wire.

Many successful entrepreneurs started with little money or formal education and, in some cases, with no background in their field of endeavor. Edison attended school for just three months and was thought to be unintelligent when he was young. Morse had been a portrait painter. Carnegie's first job was as a bobbin boy in a cotton mill. Rockefeller started out as a bookkeeper. Their humble beginnings inspired others to believe that anything was possible in America.

The fortunes made after the Civil War gave rise to large philanthropic contributions. Wealthy industrialists donated millions of dollars for libraries, schools, museums, hospitals, and other projects benefiting the general public. Carnegie Hall, a prestigious music venue in New York City, is an example of such generosity.

37
CITIES

The jobs created by large and small businesses lured Americans from rural areas to cities. Urban populations also burgeoned with millions of immigrants, many of whom came to America impoverished and unable to speak English.

For immigrants arriving in New York City after 1886, the Statue of Liberty rising out of the harbor was a majestic symbol. The monument was a gift from France to commemorate the founding of the United States and to celebrate the close relationship between the two countries. "The New Colossus," a poem by Emma Lazarus, is engraved on a plaque inside the pedestal. It ends with the words:

> Keep ancient lands, your storied pomp! cries she with silent lips.
> Give me your tired, your poor,
> Your huddled masses yearning to breathe free,
> The wretched refuse of your teeming shore.
> Send these, the homeless, tempest-tossed to me,
> I lift my lamp beside the golden door!

Twelve million immigrants were processed through nearby Ellis Island beginning in 1892.

The rapid population growth in cities put a strain on local governments and utility companies working to provide electrical power, water and sewage systems, schools, police and fire protection, and trash collection. Before the country fully transitioned away from using horses and other animals for transportation, piles of dung had to be cleared from city streets.

The urban poor typically lived in tenements. Many of these multi-level apartment buildings were run down, overcrowded, and had few windows and no indoor plumbing. Privies located in rear yards were pits of human waste. Better tenements had indoor toilets shared by multiple families.

Buildings constructed of wood and built close to or connected to one another were fire hazards. A disastrous fire in Chicago in 1871 killed 250 people and destroyed much of the downtown area.

With throngs of people cramming into cities, more indoor space was needed, but it was also important to be near the center of town. Taller buildings were the obvious solution. The first skyscraper, built in Chicago in 1885, was 10 stories high. Subsequent buildings had many more floors, but this increased traffic at the ground level. Streetcars, horse-drawn carriages, and pedestrians all competed for space on thoroughfares. To relieve congestion, large municipalities built elevated rail lines and underground subways for rapid transit through the city.

For those who could afford it, big cities offered electricity, gas for heating and cooking, hot and cold running water, telephones, and other conveniences years before they were available in the rest of the country. There were art museums, theaters, orchestras, large schools and libraries, and a variety of stores and restaurants. Cities could make rural life seem dull by comparison.

38
ORGANIZED LABOR

In the latter half of the 1800s an individual worker's demands for higher wages, more benefits, or better working conditions could be ignored by a business owner because of the seemingly inexhaustible labor pool. To give their grievances more weight, workers organized into unions, usually by trade or by industry. Union workers pay dues to support the union financially and often have to meet certain skill requirements. They vote to determine what actions to take as a group. Members accept the decisions of the majority so they can act with one voice when making demands and concessions in negotiations with business owners.

When management and labor cannot resolve disputes through negotiation, union workers can use an aggressive tactic to try to get what they want: they can strike. When employees go out on strike, they stop working and usually form picket lines at the business, carrying signs and chanting catchy phrases stating their demands. It can be dangerous for replacement workers to cross picket lines. A strike makes it difficult, sometimes impossible, for a company to continue operating. Vandalism is not uncommon.

The first nationwide strike occurred in 1877 after railroad companies cut employee wages. The violence that erupted left 100 people dead, caused millions of dollars in property damage, and paralyzed rail traffic throughout the East and Midwest. This was a new age of business, when disruptions at a company with extensive operations could affect people in multiple cities and states across the country.

The American Federation of Labor (AFL) was founded in 1886 as an umbrella group for various unions. It grew to become the most influential labor organization. Samuel Gompers was its first president and served in that post for 37 years.

39
THE GREAT PLAINS,
INDIAN WARS, and the BUFFALO

Much of the western half of the country was still open frontier when the Civil War began. To encourage settlement, in 1862 Congress passed the Homestead Act, which granted 160-acre parcels to anyone willing to live on the land for five years.

Settlers on the Great Plains encroached on the territory of Plains Indians, who depended on bison for their subsistence. Buffalo tongues, hides, robes, and bones (used to make fertilizers and china) were also valued by the non-Indian population in the country. Before the Civil War, the difficulty of transporting those commodities limited the killing of bison, but with the expansion of rail lines into the Great Plains in the 1860s and '70s, an uncontrolled slaughter of the animal commenced, in some instances just for sport.

Native Americans believed they were the rightful owners of the land and fought to stop the threats to their way of life. To enforce U.S. claims and protect travelers and settlers, the government deployed the military to round up the Plains Indians and confine them to reservations.

The army's two worst defeats in these Indian wars occurred in the northern plains. The first took place in 1866 along Wyoming's Bozeman Trail, which connected the gold mines of Montana with the Oregon Trail, the main overland route to the Pacific Northwest. Indian decoys taunted an army unit of 80 men. The commander, Captain William Fetterman, took the bait and led his troops over a ridge that concealed a thousand Lakota, Cheyenne, and Arapaho warriors. None of the soldiers survived.

Ten years later Lieutenant Colonel George Armstrong Custer, commanding a cavalry regiment of 650 soldiers, came upon a large encampment of Native Americans along the Little Bighorn River in Montana. Custer divided his regiment to make a three-pronged attack and personally led one of the groups. An overwhelming force of 1,800 Indians led by Chief Sitting Bull and Chief Crazy Horse counterattacked and annihilated Custer and his detachment of 210 soldiers along with 53 others from the regiment.

But eventually the military subdued the Plains Indians. The last major incident of armed resistance was in 1890 at Wounded Knee Creek in South Dakota. A cavalry regiment taking a band of 300 Sioux into custody was confiscating their weapons when a gun discharged. In the ensuing chaos, 30 soldiers and 200 Native Americans – men, women, and children – were killed.

By this time the buffalo was near extinction. Once numbered in the tens of millions, the population had been reduced to a thousand head.

In 1887 President Grover Cleveland signed the Dawes Act into law. It authorized the distribution of communally held tribal land to individual Indians on the reservations according to age and family status. Heads of households were allotted 160 acres. Unmarried persons received 80 acres if they were over 18 years of age or 40 acres if they were under 18. U.S. citizenship was granted to those receiving allotments. Any land left over could be retained by the tribe or sold to the federal government. The privately owned parcels had to be held for at least 25 years but could then be sold.

During the 47 years the legislation was in effect, two-thirds of Native American lands, or 103 million acres, became the property of non-Indians.

40
THE OPEN RANGE and YELLOWSTONE

The extension of rail lines into Kansas after the Civil War and an increase in demand for beef made it profitable for Texas ranchers to supply cattle to meat processing plants in Chicago and elsewhere. To reach the railroad shipping points, ranchers hired cowboys to drive their livestock hundreds of miles north over the open range. This largely unpopulated area of the Great Plains provided excellent grazing during the journey. Any unclaimed cattle found roaming freely on the prairie were rounded up, branded, and added to the herd. The number of such cattle had grown into the hundreds of thousands due to the prolonged absence of Texas ranchers and ranch hands who had been away fighting for the Confederacy.

The era of large cattle drives on the open range lasted only a couple of decades after it began around 1866. With the increase in migration to the Great Plains, settlers did not want herds passing through their land. A new invention, barbed wire, gave landowners an inexpensive fencing material to help protect their property and establish boundaries. Spikes in the twisted wire kept livestock from crossing over the fences. The well-worn cattle trails were broken up as cowboys were forced to make detours around private property.

The severe winter of 1886-87 and a disease transmitted to other cattle by Texas cattle ticks also contributed to the demise of the trails. Long cattle drives were no longer necessary after railroads expanding into Texas made it possible to transport the animals by rail all the way from the ranch to the packing house.

The lure of gold and silver continued to draw prospectors westward. Mining towns were notorious for lawlessness and vice. Butch Cassidy, Black Bart, the Dalton Gang, and other outlaws robbed local banks and shipments of gold, silver, and currency. Some towns survived after the mines gave out; others became ghost towns when everyone left.

With parts of the western half of the country rapidly being settled, the federal government set aside 2.2 million acres in 1872 for the first national park in the world. Yellowstone, located mostly in northwestern Wyoming, set a precedent for preserving places for their natural beauty, their historical, cultural, or environmental importance, or for recreation.*

* *Conservation would be a hallmark of Theodore Roosevelt's presidency. During his administration (1901-1909), the government created five national parks, four game preserves, 24 reclamation projects, 51 bird sanctuaries, 150 national forests, and 18 national monuments – 230 million acres in all.*

The federal government currently controls 635 million acres, or 28 percent of the total 2.3 billion acres in the United States. Numerous agencies administer the acreage, most of which is in the Western states and Alaska. Federal lands comprise 45 percent of California, 69 percent of Alaska, and 85 percent of Nevada.

41
EDUCATION

According to government statistics, 80 percent of the U.S. population was literate in 1870. Students attended public school an average of 78 days a year. Elementary school enrollment stood at 78 percent, but high school enrollment was less than three percent.*

Colleges and universities grew in number and enrollment after the Civil War.[†] Wealthy individuals such as Cornelius Vanderbilt, Ezra Cornell, and Leland Stanford founded or endowed private universities that bear their names. Rockefeller helped make the University of Chicago a world-class institution.

Most institutes of higher learning were not open to women or African-Americans. After the war, more schools were established specifically for them. Smith, Wellesley, and Bryn Mawr are prestigious women's colleges founded during the period. Morehouse College and Howard University were early black institutions.

The Tuskegee Institute in Alabama was another prominent school for African-Americans. Its first president, Booker T. Washington, was born into slavery. He encouraged blacks to focus on economic advancement, and social and political equality would come later. One of Tuskegee's professors, George Washington Carver, became a world-renowned scientist, agronomist, and educator.

Book publishing flourished in the postwar era. Major publishers established their headquarters in New York City. Samuel Clemens, better known by his pen name, Mark Twain, was a successful author of the time. Two of his novels, *The Adventures of Tom Sawyer* (1876) and *The Adventures of Huckleberry Finn* (1884), both set in frontier America, remained popular long after their original publication.

Newspapers were read by most Americans. Some publishers expanded their reach by acquiring newspaper companies in multiple cities. News services such as the Associated Press (AP) made it possible for even small newspapers to report timely national and international news.

Public libraries were familiar features of American towns and cities by the early 1900s. Andrew Carnegie made substantial contributions toward this effort, erecting 1,700 libraries throughout the country. A college librarian, Melville Dewey, devised a system for classifying books that became the standard.

* *The high school graduation rate reached 50 percent for the first time in 1940. The graduation rate in 2014 was 82 percent.*

† *Nine colleges were founded in the colonial era, including Harvard, Yale, and other Ivy League schools. Most were established under the auspices of certain denominations, with the education of clergy being a primary purpose. By 1860, there were 17 state universities and 229 private colleges in the country.*

42

SPORTS

The prosperity enjoyed by Americans in the late 19th century afforded more leisure time. For recreation, millions turned to spectator sports. Professional leagues organized games between teams from different cities. Fans filled stadiums to cheer on the home team.

Baseball, played in the summer, became the national pastime. Professional teams operated under the auspices of either the National League or the American League.* League champions played against each other for the first time in the 1880s. Since 1903 that contest to determine the best team in Major League Baseball has been an annual event known as the World Series.

Professional football, played in the fall, began in the 1890s but took several decades to gain a large following. Football was first popular as a college sport.

Basketball was invented in Massachusetts in 1891. James Naismith, a physical education instructor at the YMCA Training School, needed a challenging indoor game for students during the winter months between football and baseball seasons. As the game was originally conceived, players threw the ball into peach baskets hung at opposite ends of a gymnasium.

In the early days of professional boxing, opponents hit each other with their bare fists, and matches ended only when one of the two boxers was too injured to continue. In the late 1800s, American prize fighters adopted England's Queensberry rules, which made padded gloves mandatory. John L. Sullivan, "Gentleman Jim" Corbett, and Jack Johnson were early champions.

* *Blacks played in their own segregated professional baseball league for decades before Jackie Robinson broke the color barrier in the major leagues in 1947.*

43
ALASKA & HAWAII,
WAR with SPAIN, and the PANAMA CANAL

In 1867 the United States purchased Alaska from the Russians for $7.2 million. Over twice the size of Texas, this additional 375 million acres increased the size of the country by nearly 20 percent at a cost of less than 2¢ per acre. Even at that price, Alaska was generally regarded as a waste of money. In the years since, it has proved to be worth billions of dollars in natural resources alone.

Hawaii is an archipelago consisting of more than a hundred islands spread over 1,500 miles in the Pacific. The main islands lie 2,500 miles southwest of California. In the 19th century, Americans and Europeans with sugar plantations in Hawaii controlled much of the economy there. They deposed the native monarch, Queen Liliuokalani, in a bloodless coup in 1893. Five years later the United States annexed the islands despite objections from native Hawaiians.

By the 1890s, the Caribbean islands of Cuba and Puerto Rico and the Pacific islands of Guam and the Philippines were practically all that was left of Spain's once-vast overseas empire. American public opinion, influenced by sensational reporting of Spanish abuses ("yellow journalism"), favored Cuban rebels fighting for independence.

The Cuban city of Havana was a regular port of call for American naval vessels, and in January 1898 the USS *Maine* arrived. Three weeks later the battleship exploded in the harbor, killing 260 sailors. A Navy court of inquiry did not assign blame but concluded that an external marine mine had caused the disaster. It was widely believed in the U.S., though never proven conclusively, that Spaniards had sabotaged the ship.

In April 1898 the United States declared war on Spain. The Spanish-American War lasted less than four months, but America's victory produced long-term results. Cuba gained its independence* and Puerto Rico, the Philippines, and Guam became U.S. territories.†

Admiral George Dewey was hailed as a hero for having commanded a naval squadron that destroyed the Spanish fleet at the Battle of Manila Bay in the Philippines. Not one American life was lost.

The most famous soldier of the war was Theodore Roosevelt. After Congress declared war, he resigned his post as assistant secretary of the Navy and helped form a volunteer cavalry regiment. Known as the Rough Riders, the unit deployed for combat in Cuba. During the Battle of San Juan Hill, Roosevelt led a charge that destroyed enemy positions on an adjacent hill. His bravery catapulted him to high elective office – first as governor of New York, then as vice-president, and finally as president of the United States in 1901.

Before the 20th century, the only practical sea route between the Atlantic Ocean and the Pacific was around Cape Horn, at the southern tip of South America.‡ Digging a canal through the Isthmus of Panama, the strip of land connecting North and South America, had long been considered. Such a passageway through the continents would cut 8,000 miles off a voyage between New York and San Francisco.

In 1903 Colombia, which ruled Panama, rejected an American proposal to build the canal. The United States backed a revolution in Panama that enabled the people to gain their independence. The new Panamanian government accepted a treaty that gave the U.S. sovereignty over a 10-mile-wide swath of territory through the heart of the country in return for $10 million and annual payments of $250,000.

Work began the following year on what became one of the largest and most difficult engineering projects in history. The health of the workers was a major concern. American planners improved sanitation and exterminated the mosquitoes known to transmit yellow fever and malaria. In 1914 the 50-mile-long Panama Canal opened to traffic.§

---

* *During the war, the U.S. established a naval base (nicknamed Gitmo) at Guantanamo Bay in southeastern Cuba and has maintained control of the installation ever since under various treaties.*

† *The Philippines became an independent country in 1946.*

‡ *The Northwest Passage, a waterway to the Pacific Ocean through the North American continent that had been sought for centuries, was finally discovered in 1906, but it ran through northern Canada and was impractical for commercial navigation due to extreme cold and ice.*

§ *The U.S. maintained the Canal Zone for the rest of the century before ceding control to Panama on the last day of 1999.*

44

BICYCLES, AIRPLANES, and AUTOMOBILES

Bicycles were extremely popular by the late 1800s. Millions of Americans rode for both recreation and transportation. In 1903 two bicycle mechanics invented a new type of vehicle that would change the world.

Before the 20th century, people had been carried aloft in balloons, blimps, and dirigibles made lighter than air when filled with hot air or hydrogen or helium gas. The flight of such aircraft could be controlled to a certain extent, making it possible to land safely, but the principles of modern aerodynamics were not known. In 1899 Wilbur and Orville Wright, owners of a small bicycle shop in Dayton, Ohio, set out to solve those mysteries, which had perplexed scientists and engineers for centuries.

After reading everything they could find on the subject, the Wright brothers built kites and gliders to conduct their own experiments. Most of their test flights took place on the beach at Kill Devil Hills, a remote village on the Outer Banks of North Carolina. With strong winds blowing in off the ocean, high dunes from which to launch, and the somewhat-forgiving beach sand when they landed hard, it was an ideal location. By 1902 the Wrights had mastered the principles of flight in their glider.

To achieve powered flight, they needed a strong but lightweight motor and highly efficient propellers. When those could not be found, the brothers were again forced to rely on their own research and skill. They designed and built the motor and propellers themselves.

Their airplane was ready on the morning of December 17, 1903. The weather was cold and windy at Kill Devil Hills. With Orville at the controls and Wilbur running alongside, the plane rose from a flat stretch of the beach to make the first powered, controlled, and sustained flight of a heavier-than-air aircraft in history. Though it lasted only 12 seconds, did not go higher than 15 feet, and covered a distance of only 40 yards, the flight was a triumph of Yankee ingenuity and ushered in a new age in aviation. The brothers telegraphed the news of their achievement from the nearby town of Kitty Hawk.

In ground transportation, improvements to the internal combustion engine spurred innovation to replace the horse and buggy with a motorized vehicle, or "horseless carriage." Henry Ford emerged as the most successful automobile manufacturer. His hometown of Detroit, Michigan, already a commercial and transportation hub, became the center of the industry.

The Ford Motor Company began making cars in 1903, but production costs were so high that only the wealthy could afford the vehicles. That changed after Ford started using assembly lines. A car was built by different groups of workers as the chassis was conveyed down a track running the length of the plant. One group installed the engine, another group the wheels, and so on until a completed car rolled off the end of the line, ready to be sold.

Assembly lines and other innovative and efficient manufacturing techniques reduced Ford's production costs so dramatically that he was able to sell his Model T at a price most households could afford. Sales skyrocketed, but his factory workers struggled with the monotony of performing repetitive tasks. To maintain morale, Ford reduced their workday from nine hours to eight hours and more than doubled the wage of the average autoworker to the unprecedented sum of five dollars a day.

By 1917 Ford and other manufacturers had sold close to seven million motor vehicles in the United States. Towns advertised to attract tourists, and businesses catering to travelers sprang up along the highways. Federal, state, and local governments had difficulty building and maintaining roads to accommodate the rapidly increasing traffic.

45
PICTURES and RADIO

Cameras were invented before the Civil War, but they were bulky and hard to operate, even for professionals. The images were captured on glass plates. In 1888 George Eastman's company, Kodak, made picture-taking possible for amateurs by producing a small box camera that used roll film. When Kodak introduced its Brownie camera in 1900 for just one dollar, photography became available to virtually everyone.

A related industry was spawned with the invention of cameras that recorded motion and projectors that displayed those images on wide screens for viewing by large audiences. Early movies were filmed in black and white and had no sound, but people flocked to theaters, which sprang up all over the country.*

The first movie studios were built in the Northeast and Midwest, but those were not suitable locations during the winter, when harsh weather made shooting scenes outdoors difficult, if not impossible. Furthermore, sunlight was required to expose the film properly because electric lights of the period were not bright enough. Filmmakers found an ideal climate in the Southern California town of Hollywood.

Radio, an even bigger form of mass communication, made wireless transmission into homes possible. By the 1920s broadcast companies were producing news and entertainment programs to compete for listeners and advertisers. Broadcasts were free to anyone with a radio within range of the signal.

* *Movies with spoken dialogue ("talkies") were introduced in the 1920s. By the '30s music, sound effects, and color were additional features incorporated into commercially successful feature films.*

<hr>

46
PROGRESSIVISM

Industrial growth after the Civil War fueled a rise in the standard of living, and huge fortunes were amassed by some, but significant societal problems developed. Mark Twain called the era a Gilded Age, not a golden one. The wealth that was created masked abuses and struggles of the less fortunate. "Muckraking" journalists sought to expose the ills: the power of monopolies, the mistreatment of workers, the plight of the poor, and the selling of harmful products. Progressivism, the movement to correct these and other problems, rejected laissez-faire capitalism in favor of increased government intervention.

Monopolies and trusts were large companies that stifled and, in some instances, eliminated competition. Congress passed the Sherman Antitrust Act in 1890 and the Clayton Antitrust Act in 1914 to break up monopolies and keep new ones from forming. The enforcement of these laws was known as trustbusting. The government created the Interstate Commerce Commission and the Federal Trade Commission to monitor business practices and encourage competition.

The decennial census taken in the year 1900 classified approximately two million children as laborers. Some held jobs instead of going to school. Children could be found working long hours and even through the night in unsafe conditions. Legislation passed in 1916 and 1919 to address the problem was struck down by the Supreme Court as unconstitutional.*

The Jungle, a 1906 novel by Upton Sinclair, sensationalized unsanitary conditions in the meat packing industry. The public outcry led to passage of the Pure Food and Drug Act, which made it unlawful to manufacture, sell, or distribute food products or medicines that were harmful or did not have accurate labels on the packaging.

In 1912 voters elected Woodrow Wilson as the 28th president of the United States. He urged legislators to reduce tariffs and levy a tax on personal incomes.

The country's first income tax, imposed in 1862 during the Civil War, lasted only 10 years. It was revived in 1894, but the Supreme Court declared it unconstitutional the following year. The 16th Amendment, ratified in 1913, removed the constitutional obstacle, and the federal government instituted a tax on personal incomes later that year.[†] A tax on corporate incomes had been imposed four years earlier. Income taxes have been a permanent fixture of the U.S. tax code ever since and currently account for over half of all federal revenue. They are administered by the Internal Revenue Service (IRS), a bureau of the Treasury Department.

Income taxes are said to be progressive because tax rates increase as income rises. In other words, individuals and corporations with higher taxable incomes generally pay a greater percentage of their income in taxes, up to a maximum rate.[‡]

President Wilson also signed the Federal Reserve Act into law in 1913. The legislation revamped currency laws and instituted a central banking system with 12 regional federal banks. The Federal Reserve Board exercises broad powers in controlling credit and regulating the flow of money. As the "lender of last resort," it can provide emergency loans to financial institutions to help stabilize the economy during a crisis. The agency is subject to congressional oversight, but by and large, it is an independent body within the government.

---

* *In 1938 lawmakers passed the Fair Labor Standards Act, and the courts upheld its restrictions on child labor.*

† *Since 1943 personal income taxes have been collected primarily through payroll deductions. Employers withhold a specified amount from the paychecks of their workers for estimated income taxes and remit the money to the federal government on behalf of their employees. Individuals are required to calculate the exact amount owed for the calendar year and submit the results on forms designed by the government. The deadline for filing individual income tax returns for the prior year is April 15. If taxpayers owe more, they must pay the additional amount by that date to avoid a penalty. If too much tax was withheld, the Department of the Treasury refunds the difference. Most states impose a separate state income tax.*

‡ *The highest corporate income tax rate in 2015 was 39 percent. The highest individual rate was 39.6 percent. Those with adjusted gross incomes in the top 20 percent paid 87 percent of the federal income taxes collected. Seventy-eight million American households with lesser incomes, or 45 percent of the total, paid no federal income tax. In 1990 the figure was 21 percent.*

47

WORLD WAR I

Events in Europe overshadowed progressive reforms in America. In 1914 a young revolutionary assassinated the Austrian archduke, Francis Ferdinand, and his wife during their visit to Serbia, a country in southeastern Europe. In the ensuing uproar, the nations of Europe honored their alliances, which embroiled most of the continent and eventually much of the world in a war. On one side were the Allies, which included France, Great Britain, Russia, Italy, Japan, and Serbia. Their enemies, known as the Central Powers, were Germany, Austria-Hungary, Turkey, and Bulgaria. For the first years of the war, the United States remained officially neutral, although American firms favored the Allies in terms of exports and bank loans.

In the early stages, neither the Allies nor the Central Powers gained the upper hand. As a stalemate developed, armies on both sides dug trenches for protection from enemy guns and artillery. Soldiers ventured out of the trenches only sporadically to fight. Charging the enemy, a common tactic in earlier wars, was much more dangerous in World War I* because of land mines, barbed wire, and machine guns that could fire continuously.

To break the impasse, the combatants introduced poison gas as a weapon. The gases caused burns and blisters on the skin, blindness upon contact with the eyes, and death if inhaled. Soldiers were given gas masks for protection but were often unable to don the masks before succumbing to the poison.

The British invented the tank, an armed and motorized track vehicle that could cross through barbed wire and over trenches. Airplanes modified for warfare shot down military balloons and dirigibles and engaged in bombing, reconnaissance, and aerial "dogfights" with enemy aircraft.

At sea, both sides tried to keep supplies from getting through to their adversaries. Germany's use of submarines, or "undersea boats," was extremely effective. U-boats could launch torpedoes and then withdraw without ever being seen. Deck guns gave them the capability of attacking from the surface. U-boats were dreaded weapons that sent close to 5,000 Allied and neutral ships to the bottom of the ocean.

In 1915 an English ocean liner, the *Lusitania*, was returning from New York when it went down off the coast of Ireland, sunk by a single U-boat torpedo. Twelve hundred passengers, including 128 Americans, died in the attack. While expressing regret for the loss of life, Germany defended the action because the liner's cargo included munitions destined for use against German soldiers. Americans were out-raged. To appease the United States, Germany pledged not to attack passenger liners without warning in the future, but maintained the right to search commercial vessels. If war supplies were found, a ship would be confiscated or sunk, but non-combatants would not be harmed.

Diplomacy kept the U.S. out of the war for the time being. Americans did not want to become more involved in battles being fought in Europe. The Atlantic Ocean served as a protective buffer. Nevertheless, the United States prepared to enter the conflict if necessary.[†]

Germany's efforts to form an alliance with Mexico against the U.S. came to light in January 1917. In February, Germany reneged on its earlier pledge and returned to unrestricted submarine warfare, sinking several American merchant ships over the next two months. President Wilson went to Capitol Hill in April seeking a declaration of war to make the world "safe for democracy." Congress declared war on Germany a few days later. War was declared on Austria-Hungary in December. The United States did not declare war on the other Central Powers. Turkey and Bulgaria were not seen as direct threats, and the U.S. did not want to jeopardize its relations in the region.

---

* *At the time, the conflict was called the Great War because many countries and millions of troops were engaged. After war broke out across the world again in 1939, it became more common to refer to the Great War as World War I.*

† *U.S. preparations to enter the war included the $25 million purchase of the Danish Virgin Islands in 1916 to prevent Germany from acquiring those Caribbean islands for a naval base.*

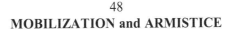

48
MOBILIZATION and ARMISTICE

America's troop strength was under 200,000 the year before its entry into World I. To quickly build up a military force of sufficient size, Congress instituted a draft. Close to three million men were conscripted into the armed services. With the addition of volunteers, National Guard troops, and reservists called up to active duty, a total of 4.7 million Americans would serve during the war.

Production in the U.S. shifted to the war effort. The federal government set maximum prices for industrial goods such as steel and rubber. Food supplies, as essential as military equipment, were increased by discouraging waste, encouraging cutbacks in public consumption, and mandating high minimum prices for wheat to encourage farmers to grow more.

Delivering raw materials and manufactured goods where they were needed was a huge task. The government ordered the construction of more rail cars and locomotives and put the railroads under federal control to keep freight from bogging down in competing rail lines. Transporting equipment and supplies across the Atlantic to the war zone was a bigger problem. More ships were built. To get past German U-boats, cargo vessels and troop transports sailed close together in convoys escorted by warships.

American troops under the command of General John J. Pershing began arriving in France in June 1917. The enemy launched a series of attacks in the spring of 1918, hoping to win the war before more reinforcements could be brought up. German troops advanced to within 50 miles of Paris, but Allied forces held the line and went on the offensive. A million U.S. soldiers were engaged along the Meuse-Argonne front in northeastern France. Fighting was fierce in the dense woods, deep ravines, and heavy fog of the Argonne Forest.

American forces provided a great boost to the Allies and helped overwhelm the exhausted enemy. Resistance from the Central Powers collapsed in the fall of 1918. Germany, the last to give up, agreed to an armistice, or cessation of fighting, that went into effect at the 11th hour on the 11th day of the 11th month (November).

More than 116,000 American servicemen died in the war, and 204,000 were wounded. Their sacrifice made the Allied victory possible.

After the fighting stopped, Allied leaders met to formulate separate terms of surrender for each of the Central Powers. Some people believed the Great War would be "the war to end all wars." President Wilson set forth 14 policies he believed would bring about a lasting peace. For the most part, Allied leaders rejected his plan. The Treaty of Versailles forced Germany to give up territory, accept full responsibility for causing the war, and pay steep reparations to compensate the Allies for their losses. Germans bitterly resented the terms, which sowed the seeds of a more destructive global conflict just two decades later.

The last of President Wilson's Fourteen Points called for the formation of an international organization to help resolve disputes. The proposal was written into the Treaty of Versailles, but the U.S. Senate did not approve the treaty. The League of Nations was created in 1920 and met regularly until 1946, but the United States never became a member.

49

EPIDEMIC, GANGSTERS,
WOMEN'S SUFFRAGE, and IMMIGRATION

The worldwide death toll from the First World War was at least 15 million, counting civilians and military personnel. A flu virus in 1918 and 1919 took even more lives in one of the worst epidemics in history. In the United States, a quarter of the population contracted the disease, and more than 600,000 died – 196,000 in the month of October 1918 alone. Many expired within hours of becoming infected. Young and middle-aged adults showed an unusually high susceptibility.

A period known as Prohibition began in 1919 with ratification of the 18th Amendment, which banned the manufacture, sale, or distribution of alcoholic beverages. Those who ignored the law were called bootleggers. Some outlaws involved in bootlegging and other illegal activities banded together and maintained their criminal enterprises through extortion, bribery, and murder. Al Capone, based in Chicago, was a notorious gangster of the period.*

The Constitution was amended again in 1920. The 19th Amendment prohibited the denial or abridgement of voting rights based on sex. The movement to secure the right to vote (also called suffrage or the franchise) and other freedoms for women began before the Civil War and was an outgrowth of the fight to abolish slavery. Lucretia Mott and Elizabeth Cady Stanton were among the leaders who organized the first women's rights convention at Seneca Falls, New York, in 1848. Other reformers such as Susan B. Anthony, Carrie Chapman Catt, and Alice Paul advanced the movement that eventually achieved nationwide female suffrage.[†]

In the aftermath of World War I, a flood of immigrants fled war-torn Europe for America. Most came from southern and eastern Europe. There was a backlash in the United States and a rise in nativism, the favoring of existing residents over newcomers. In 1921 President Warren G. Harding signed the Emergency Quota Act, the nation's first quantitative immigration law. It limited the annual number of new immigrants of any nationality to three percent of their foreign-born countrymen already residing in the U.S. Exceptions were made for the children of American citizens and for immigrants from the Western Hemisphere.

Two hundred thousand African-American soldiers served in France during the First World War. They returned home wanting the same respect they had received overseas. Members of the revived Ku Klux Klan tried to prevent that. Meeting at night in ritualistic outdoor gatherings, Klan members dressed in white robes, wore hoods to hide their faces, and burned crosses. Through violence, including murder, the KKK sought to intimidate blacks and keep them from seeking greater opportunity in society. Catholics and Jews were also targets of the Klan.

Southern blacks had begun relocating to cities in the North in large numbers prior to World War I. That trend continued after the war. From 1910 to 1930 more than a million people were part of this Great Migration. The transition was often difficult because of low-paying jobs, housing in run-down neighborhoods, and racism. Race riots flared up in several Northern cities, most notably in East St. Louis, Illinois, in 1917.

* *The 21st Amendment, ratified in 1933, repealed the 18th Amendment and ended Prohibition.*

† *Some states and territories in the U.S. allowed women to vote prior to the 19th Amendment.*

50
THE JAZZ AGE

The 1920s are often referred to as the Roaring Twenties or the Jazz Age. Jazz, a uniquely American musical genre that became popular in the decade, grew out of the spirituals and work songs of slaves. Louis Armstrong, a trumpet player who also sang, was an early pioneer. The Charleston was a dance inspired by the music.

The author who best symbolized the period was F. Scott Fitzgerald. Ernest Hemingway and William Faulkner were also recognized as important literary figures. The playwright Eugene O'Neill won three Pulitzer Prizes in the decade. Two magazines first published in the Twenties, *Reader's Digest* and *Time*, still have wide circulations.

In 1927 American aviator Charles Lindbergh collected a $25,000 prize and became an international hero after making the first nonstop transatlantic flight between New York and Paris. The historic crossing took 33½ hours in his small single-engine airplane, the *Spirit of St. Louis*.

The overall U.S. economy grew in the '20s, but serious problems developed. Farm incomes declined because of overproduction and a drop in foreign demand for American agricultural products after World War I. Businesses and individuals took on too much debt. Banks and brokerages overextended themselves with risky loans, some of which were used to speculate in the stock market, the means by which shares of publicly traded companies are bought and sold. There are a number of facilities for trading stocks in the United States. The largest is the New York Stock Exchange located on Wall Street in New York City.

When people buy stock or shares in a company, they become part-owners, although the individual percentage is usually relatively small. Shareholders make a profit if the company pays dividends* or if the stock is sold for more than the purchase price. A loss is realized when shares are sold for less than the purchase price. A company's stock price often drops if sales or profits do not meet expectations, but other factors can affect the value as well.

In the 1920s investors bid share prices to record highs. The Dow Jones Industrial Average, an important stock market index, multiplied in value by a factor of six during the decade.

cash payments made by a company to its shareholders

51
THE GREAT DEPRESSION

Market economies are cyclical; they expand and contract. In the course of the long-term upward trend, the United States economy experienced several severe downturns in the 19th century beginning in 1807, 1837, 1873, and 1893, respectively. Each depression lasted for years.

The worst contraction of all, the Great Depression, occurred in the 20th century and lasted for a decade. It began in October 1929 when plummeting stock prices spread panic across the country. Consumers cut back on purchases. Businesses laid off workers* or reduced the wages of those kept on the payroll. There was a run on banks as bank customers, in need of cash and worried about the security of their deposits, tried to withdraw all their money. Many banks ran out of cash.

Banks do not keep on hand all the money their customers deposit. Most of it is loaned out to businesses and individuals and invested in stocks, bonds, and other securities. Like everyone else with stock market investments, banks lost money in the crash. And bank customers defaulted on loans. Unable to withstand such reversals, more than 9,000 banks, a third of the total in the country, went out of business between 1930 and 1933.

Families lost homes when they could no longer pay their mortgages. In some cities the homeless set up shacks in empty fields. These shantytowns were called "Hoovervilles" by those who blamed President Herbert Hoover for the bad economy. People in large cities who did not have money to buy food stood in long lines to get free meals of soup and bread provided by charities and the government.

In general, the federal government responded poorly, increasing the severity and duration of the crisis. The Federal Reserve did not shore up the banking system when the money supply was contracting. Taxes were increased. High tariffs inhibited foreign trade.

Entertainment helped people cope with the hardships. Americans listened to radio programs and music recordings. With ticket prices as low as 10¢, movies remained popular during the difficult times.

* *The unemployment rate during the Great Depression peaked at 25 percent in 1933 and was still high, 19 percent, in 1938.*

52
NEW DEAL

The presidential election of 1932 came three years into the Great Depression. President Hoover was soundly defeated by Franklin Delano Roosevelt, a distant cousin of the former president, Theodore Roosevelt. Often referred to by his initials, FDR told the nation in his inaugural address that "the only thing we have to fear is fear itself." In "fireside chats" broadcast over the radio, President Roosevelt tried to reassure Americans that the worst was behind them and the government was working to help solve the nation's problems. His optimism was contagious. The fact that he was crippled from polio and could not walk was not widely publicized.

Under Roosevelt's plan, called the New Deal, the federal government implemented numerous economic reforms.

There was widespread distrust of banks because people had lost money when their banks failed.* The president signed legislation creating the Federal Deposit Insurance Corporation (FDIC), an agency that guaranteed the safety of customer bank accounts up to certain limits.

Investors were the first to be hurt by the economic collapse.[†] To rebuild trust in the financial markets, the Securities and Exchange Commission (SEC) was created to punish fraud and regulate stock and bond transactions.

To reduce unemployment, the federal government funded and managed public works projects such as the construction of roads, bridges, schools, airports, hospitals, parks, and housing for the poor. The Tennessee Valley Authority (TVA) was created to build dams for flood control and to harness waterpower for cheaper electricity in the South. Out West, the Hoover Dam was completed on the Colorado River and construction began on the Grand Coulee Dam on the Columbia River.

The government paid farmers to grow less and, in some cases, to destroy existing farm produce and livestock. The reduction in supply caused food prices to rise, which increased farm incomes. Farmers also benefited from the extension of electric power to rural areas.

The Great Depression was particularly hard on farmers on the Great Plains. The soil had deteriorated due to shortsighted agricultural practices and a drought that began in 1931. When strong winds blew across the Plains states in 1933, the topsoil was carried away in giant dust storms that made the region a "Dust Bowl" unsuitable for farming. Many families had no alternative but to pack up and leave.

The federal government instituted Social Security in 1937. Payments made under the program were intended to provide a safety net to the poor, the elderly, the disabled, and the unemployed.[‡]

In 1938 Congress passed a labor law that reduced the standard workweek to 40 hours and guaranteed a minimum wage of 25¢ an hour. The law also set minimum ages for employment and limited the hours children could work.

* *Customers of failed banks lost an average of 20¢ of every dollar on deposit.*

† *The stock market bottomed out in 1932 at 11 percent of its 1929 high. The market did not recover its value lost in the Great Depression until 1954, 25 years after the crash.*

‡ *The bulk of Social Security benefits are now regarded as entitlements to those who reach the standard retirement age of 65 (62 for early retirement). The expenditures account for 24 percent of the federal budget. To fund the program, a 12.4 percent tax is assessed on payrolls and self-employment income. The tax burden is borne equally by employers and employees. For employees, the tax is deducted from their paychecks at 6.2 percent of gross earnings. The self-employed pay both portions. As a result of the aging U.S. population, the ratio of contributors to beneficiaries is currently 2.8 to one.*

The taxes collected and the interest earned on that money go into Social Security trust funds, which have grown every year since 1982 because the taxes and interest were more than the benefits paid out. Since 2010, the benefits paid out have exceeded the taxes collected, but with interest earned on the accumulated reserves, the funds have continued to grow despite the shortfall. According to government projections, however, starting in 2019 the annual interest earned will no longer be sufficient to cover the deficit, and the reserves will have to be tapped. By 2034 the Social Security trust funds will be depleted.

53

WORLD WAR II

In the latter half of the 1930s the specter of another world war loomed. Italy attacked Ethiopia in 1935. Two years later the Empire of Japan went to war with China. The most ominous threat emerged in Germany. Adolph Hitler's National Socialist (Nazi) party gained control of the government and rebuilt the military. In fiery speeches Hitler fanned the resentment Germans felt about their treatment after World War I and called for revenge. He told ethnic Germans they were a superior Aryan* race destined to rule the world for a thousand years. He incited hatred and persecution of Jews, who were terrorized, rounded up and sent to prison, or killed.

In 1936 Hitler violated the Treaty of Versailles by sending troops into the Rhineland. That region along the Rhine River was supposed to remain free of militarization after World War I and serve as a buffer between the rest of Germany and neighboring countries to the west, but Allied nations acquiesced to the incursion.

Over the next three years, Germany annexed Austria, the Sudetenland (a part of Czechoslovakia inhabited by ethnic Germans), and then all of Czechoslovakia. Diplomatic efforts to halt the aggression ended in September of 1939 when Germany invaded Poland. Britain, France, and other countries, finally convinced that Hitler could be stopped only by force, declared war on Germany. World War II had begun.

The German military moved across the continent in swift attacks they called *blitzkrieg*. Denmark, Norway, Belgium, and Holland quickly fell to the onslaught. France was defeated with help from Germany's fascist ally, Italy. By the summer of 1940 most of the European mainland was under German or Italian control.

England was Germany's next target. Hoping to bomb the country into submission or weaken its defenses in preparation for an amphibious invasion, Hitler sent his air force, the *Luftwaffe*, across the English Channel both day and night. The air raids killed more than 40,000, but British Prime Minister Winston Churchill vowed never to surrender. The greatly outnumbered Royal Air Force lost 500 airmen and 1,000 planes in the Battle of Britain, but Germany lost 2,700 airmen and 1,900 planes. Hitler canceled plans for an invasion with ground troops.

The United States did not enter the war for more than two years after it began. Most Americans were isolationists, but those sentiments gradually changed as the international situation worsened.

President Roosevelt prepared the country to assume a leading role and be "the great arsenal of democracy." In 1940 he persuaded Congress to pass the first conscription in U.S. history when the nation was not at war. In March of the following year, he authorized the seizure of German and Italian ships docked in American ports. That same month Congress passed the Lend-Lease Act, which gave the president authority to provide arms and other aid to countries whose defense was deemed vital to the United States. American merchant ships and seamen transporting those supplies abroad and naval escorts providing protection risked being attacked by German submarines and aircraft.

In June 1941 Germany invaded the Soviet Union[†] in violation of their mutual non-aggression pact. America responded to this major escalation of the war by sending aid to Russia, but it would be an event later that year in the Pacific, not Europe, that drew the United States into the war as a combatant.

* *a supposed master race of non-Jewish Caucasians ideally having Nordic features*

† *After communist revolutionaries toppled the Russian monarchy in 1917 during World War I, new governments arose in the various regions of the former empire. In 1922 they came together to form a new nation, the Union of Soviet Socialist Republics (U.S.S.R.), also known as the Soviet Union or Russia, the largest of the republics. The government's headquarters, the Kremlin, sat in the heart of Moscow, Russia.*

54
PEARL HARBOR

Japan, an island nation with limited natural resources, had to import raw materials and equipment to supply its military; 80 percent of its oil came from America. Japan's continued aggression on the Asian mainland prompted the U.S. to restrict the sale of arms and other strategic goods in 1940. After Japan formed an alliance with Germany and Italy, the United States sent military aid to China under the Lend-Lease program. When Japanese troops moved into southern Indochina in July 1941, President Roosevelt froze Japanese assets in America and restricted, then cut off, oil sales.

The strained relations were finally severed on Sunday, December 7, 1941, when carrier-based Japanese aircraft attacked five U.S. military installations on the Hawaiian island of Oahu, in particular, the naval base at Pearl Harbor. The two-hour raid killed 2,335 American troops and 68 civilians, wounded 1,178, destroyed or damaged 347 aircraft, and crippled the U.S. Pacific Fleet. President Roosevelt called it "a date which will live in infamy." Congress declared war on Japan the next day and declared war on Germany and Italy three days later.

Two months after Pearl Harbor, Roosevelt issued an executive order authorizing the relocation and internment of men, women, and children of German, Italian, and Japanese descent living in the United States. Ethnic Japanese residents along the Pacific Coast of the American mainland bore the brunt of the policy. The government uprooted more than 110,000 people, most of whom were U.S. citizens, and confined them to remote camps farther inland during the war.* For a time, Japanese-Americans were prohibited from enlisting in the military and were ineligible for the draft. Those already serving were reassigned to segregated units, given menial tasks, and had their weapons taken away.[†]

* *In 1948 the federal government paid some compensation to those affected by the internment policy. President Reagan signed legislation in 1988 that formally apologized for the government's actions and gave $20,000 to surviving internees.*

[†] *The policies were later modified, and 33,000 Japanese-Americans eventually served in the U.S. armed forces during World War II. Many saw combat, mostly in segregated units in Europe. Eight hundred gave their lives.*

55
ALLIES versus AXIS

The "Big Three" Allied nations that fought in World War II were the U.S., Great Britain, and the U.S.S.R. Their respective leaders were Roosevelt, Churchill, and Joseph Stalin. The three main enemy or Axis countries were Germany, Italy, and Japan. They were led by Hitler, Benito Mussolini, and Emperor Hirohito.

The war was fought in two large geographic areas or theaters – against the Japanese in Asia and the Pacific islands (Pacific Theater) and against the Germans and Italians in North Africa and Europe (European Theater). The Allies made defeating Germany the top priority.

Industrial production in the U.S. increased dramatically to support the war. The government imposed a moratorium on the manufacture of cars, appliances, and other consumer items deemed non-essential. Even the purchase of essentials was limited. Meat, sugar, canned food, shoes, tires, and gasoline were rationed to the general public so the armed forces would have adequate supplies. The government also imposed wage and price controls.

The urgent need for military equipment and personnel ended the unemployment problem that had plagued the country for a decade. Businesses recruited women to fill positions vacated by men going off to war.* Incomes rose. Taxes were raised to offset increased military spending, but even with that, Americans had extra money and much of it went into savings accounts and war bonds (personal loans to the government to help finance the war).

German submarine attacks hampered the buildup of Allied forces in the European Theater. Often working in coordinated groups or "wolf packs," U-boats sank 3,000 ships, many of them in the Gulf of Mexico, the Caribbean, and along the East Coast of the United States. The Allies armed their merchant ships, increased the number of airplanes and warships accompanying convoys across the Atlantic, and outfitted more naval vessels with sonar, a technology used to find submerged enemy submarines. Radar and intercepted German radio transmissions helped planes and ships locate U-boats when they surfaced. The Allies also benefited from having deciphered Enigma, the secret code used by Germany to encrypt messages. As a result of these measures, U-boats became less of a threat.

In November 1942, U.S. forces joined the Allies already fighting in North Africa. They drove out the Germans and Italians the following year. Attention then turned to the liberation of Europe, which began with an Allied invasion of Italy. Fighting was fierce on the beachhead at Anzio. In June of 1944 Rome was liberated from the Germans. Mussolini had already been deposed, and the new Italian government had switched its allegiance to the Allies.†

---

* *More than 350,000 women enlisted in the U.S. military during World War II and served in every branch. They were nurses, pilots, gunnery instructors, clerks, truck drivers, and mechanics. Most were stationed in the United States, and those who went overseas were assigned non-combat duties. Nevertheless, 432 female service members died, 16 killed as a result of enemy action. Eighty-eight women were captured and held as prisoners of war.*

† *Italians loyal to the Nazis and Mussolini opposed the new government, and a civil war broke out that lasted until the end of the war. Mussolini was executed by Italian opponents in 1945 after he was caught trying to escape to neutral Switzerland.*

56
D-DAY

As Allied forces were building up in England, American and British planes struck German positions on the Continent, including in Germany itself. The Allies lost 160,000 airmen in the campaign but eventually dominated the skies. By the middle of 1944, Allied troops were prepared to liberate France and the rest of Europe. The supreme commander of Allied forces in Europe, U.S. General Dwight D. Eisenhower, ordered the long-awaited assault to begin on the morning of June 6, 1944, designated by the military as D-Day.

The Germans expected the Allies to cross the English Channel at its narrowest point. Instead the invasion, codenamed Operation Overlord, took place a few hundred miles to the south, in the Normandy region of France. The Allies divided a 60-mile stretch of French coastline into five sectors. Aircraft and warships pounded German coastal batteries as more than 3,500 landing craft carried soldiers, equipment, and supplies ashore. Other troops were dropped behind the beaches by parachute and glider. It was the largest invasion force in history.

Establishing beachheads was perilous, especially in the sector codenamed Omaha Beach, where German machine guns and artillery mowed down U.S. soldiers. Yet within hours the Atlantic Wall, coastal fortifications years under construction and touted by the Nazis as impenetrable, had been breached.

Twenty-five hundred Americans died on the first day of the Normandy Invasion. That evening, President Roosevelt led the nation in a solemn six-minute prayer broadcast over the radio.

In less than a month, a million troops had landed on French soil. As they liberated areas held by the Germans, Allied soldiers discovered numerous concentration camps where an untold number of prisoners, mostly civilians, had been tortured and killed. The Nazis had conducted medical experiments on prisoners. In some of the camps, women and girls had their heads shaved before they were killed. The hair was shipped to Axis manufacturers and used to make felt and yarn. Gold dental fillings removed from the mouths of the dead went into the German treasury.

In labor camps, many prisoners forced to work with little food eventually died from exhaustion, disease, or abuse. Other prisons were death camps designed to quickly and systematically kill en masse. The victims, among them children and the handicapped, were assembled in large groups and shot dead or stripped of their clothes and herded into rooms that were then filled with poison gas.

The genocide was on such a colossal scale that burying all the dead individually was impossible. The Germans resorted to burning the corpses in large ovens or in open pits. More than a million people were killed at the Auschwitz extermination camp in Poland. Nearly as many died at the Treblinka camp, also in Poland. An estimated six million Jews perished in the Holocaust along with up to 20 million from other ethnic groups, including Ukrainians, Russians, Poles, and Yugoslavians.

In December of 1944 Hitler launched a last, desperate offensive to stop the Allied advance. At the Battle of the Bulge, U.S. forces suffered approximately 80,000 casualties, making the month-long engagement the bloodiest of the entire war. After beating back the assault, American and British troops raced toward Berlin from the west. The Russian army, approaching from the east, entered the German capital first. Adolph Hitler committed suicide before he could be captured or killed. When Germany surrendered on May 8, 1945, Allied nations throughout the world celebrated V-E Day (Victory-in-Europe).

President Roosevelt did not live to see the defeat of Germany. He died a month earlier, after beginning a fourth term in office. He had been president since 1933.* The vice-president, Harry S. Truman, was sworn in as president.

The war was not yet over. Fighting continued in the Pacific Theater against the Japanese.

The precedent of serving no more than two presidential terms was set by George Washington and followed by every president until FDR. The 22nd Amendment, ratified in 1951, limited future presidents to two elected terms under normal succession. Members of the U.S. Congress are not subject to term limits.

57
WAR in the PACIFIC

After they attacked Pearl Harbor, the Japanese swept across Southeast Asia and the Pacific. In the Philippines 12,000 American troops and 60,000 Filipino troops on the Bataan peninsula surrendered in April of 1942. Their removal to a prison camp 65 miles away is remembered as the Bataan Death March because of the atrocities committed by the Japanese. At least 600 Americans and 5,000 Filipinos died before reaching the camp. Thousands more would die during their captivity. On the Philippine island fortress of Corregidor, 11,000 U.S. and Filipino soldiers held out for another month before they, too, were taken prisoner. The surrender of the Philippines remains the largest capitulation of U.S. forces in history.

That same April, less than five months after Pearl Harbor, sixteen American B-25 bombers took off from the aircraft carrier USS *Hornet* steaming 700 miles off the coast of Japan. Led by Lieutenant Colonel Jimmy Doolittle, the squadron bombed targets in six Japanese cities, including the capital of Tokyo. One of the planes was extremely low on fuel after the raid and diverted to Russia, where the crew was taken into custody after landing. The rest of the planes headed toward airfields controlled by Chinese allies as planned, but none had sufficient fuel. The airmen bailed out over other parts of China, crash landed, or ditched in the ocean just off the coast. Chinese soldiers and citizens protected the Americans despite an intense search by the Japanese military that left thousands of Chinese dead. All but seven of the 80 Doolittle Raiders eventually made it to safety. For his valor and leadership "above the call of duty," Doolittle was awarded the Congressional Medal of Honor, the highest military decoration given by the United States.

The results of the daring daytime attack were incalculable and extended far beyond the mission itself. It boosted American morale at a time when the outlook was bleak, and it proved that the enemy was not invincible. Moreover, the fear of another such attack caused the Japanese to hold back aircraft to protect their homeland when those planes could have been used against the Allies on the war's front lines.

Japan's advance across the Pacific was finally halted near New Guinea and Australia in May 1942 at the Battle of the Coral Sea. The next major battle took place 3,000 miles to the northeast at Midway, a tiny American atoll in the Central Pacific. The Japanese were unaware that their secret code used to encrypt messages had been deciphered.* U.S. commanders knew from intercepted communications that Japan intended to attack the remote American outpost. The ensuing battle cost the Japanese four aircraft carriers, a navy cruiser, 300 aircraft, and 3,000 sailors and pilots, losses from which they never fully recovered.

The Battle of Midway was a turning point, but the enemy remained formidable throughout most of the Pacific. The U.S. devised a brilliant plan to skip over islands where the Japanese were entrenched and attack islands that were more vulnerable. The strategy, known as "island hopping" or "leapfrogging," cut off the enemy's supply lines, leaving their strongholds to "wither on the vine."

Under the command of General Douglas MacArthur, Admiral Chester Nimitz, and Admiral William "Bull" Halsey, U.S. forces gained control of one island chain after another: the Solomon Islands, Gilbert Islands, Marshall Islands, and the Marianas. American submarines sank 1,300 Japanese warships and merchant vessels. Carriers that could launch a hundred planes helped the United States gain air superiority.

In October 1944 the campaign to retake the Philippines began with the Battle of Leyte Gulf, the largest naval engagement in history. The Japanese navy was defeated so decisively that it ceased to be a significant threat for the remainder of the war.

As the war front moved closer to their homeland, desperate Japanese commanders sent 4,000 pilots on suicidal *kamikaze* missions to crash their aircraft into U.S. ships. The attacks killed 5,000 American sailors, wounded just as many, and sank at least 34 ships and damaged another 300.

Land battles were also extremely costly because Japanese soldiers often fought to the last man. Six thousand U.S. Marines died taking the small island of Iwo Jima. Twelve thousand American troops were killed at the Battle of Okinawa.

* *Neither the Japanese nor the Germans were ever able to decipher secret U.S. messages relayed by American Indian military personnel in their native languages. Most "code talkers" were Navajo.*

58
SECRET WEAPON

By July 1945 the Allies had advanced across the Pacific to Japan itself. Planes and battleships bombarded the country repeatedly, but the Japanese would not surrender even though their defeat was inevitable. Millions of military and civilian casualties were expected should an amphibious invasion of Japan become necessary to end the war.

Since the beginning of hostilities, the U.S. had been working intensely on the Manhattan Project, a top-secret program to develop a new type of weapon more powerful and destructive than anything in history: the atom bomb. Once the bomb was successfully tested, the enemy was given an ultimatum: surrender or face annihilation. After the imperial government of Japan refused to yield, President Truman gave the order for the military to use the weapon.

On August 6, 1945, an American B-29 bomber, nicknamed *Enola Gay*, dropped an atom bomb on Hiroshima, a major port and military headquarters in southwestern Japan. The entire city was obliterated. Approximately 45,000 people died the first day. Twenty-five thousand more were fatally injured, but the Japanese did not give up.

Three days later the U.S. dropped an atom bomb on Nagasaki, the site of a large steel and armament factory. The explosion, billowing up in a mushroom cloud, destroyed that city as well and proved to be the final blow. Japan surrendered on August 14, or V-J Day (Victory-over-Japan).*

Spontaneous celebrations erupted around the world when the end of the war was announced. In cities throughout the United States, people gathered in the streets to dance and cheer. Families and friends anxiously awaited the homecoming of the men and women in the armed forces, but 405,000 American soldiers, sailors, airmen, and marines would not return. The war had cost 60 million lives worldwide.

After the war, the Allies prosecuted high-ranking Axis leaders for the suffering, death, and destruction they had caused. Eleven Nazis were executed following their trials in Nuremberg, Germany; others were imprisoned. A similar tribunal in Tokyo found seven Japanese officials guilty of war crimes and sentenced them to death. Emperor Hirohito, however, was allowed to remain as a figurehead.

To help keep the peace, countries across the globe came together to create the United Nations (U.N.) two months after the war's end. In contrast with America's stance toward the League of Nations following World War I, the United States was the principal supporter of this new international organization, headquartered in New York City.

* *The formal Japanese surrender took place on September 2, 1945, aboard the battleship USS* Missouri *anchored in Tokyo Bay.*

59
BABY BOOM, MARSHALL PLAN, and ISRAEL

A sharp increase in the U.S. birth rate followed the return of 16 million members of the military to civilian life after World War II. The "baby boom generation" would have an immense impact on the economy and on society in general for decades.

Other factors also contributed to the tremendous economic growth that followed the nation's shift back to peacetime production:

- The war's destruction had not reached the U.S. mainland.

- There was pent-up demand after a decade of economic depression and four years of wartime rationing.

- Americans had extra money to spend. Jobs had been plentiful during the war, and the savings rate was high.

- Wartime research led to new technologies and new products.

- Workers became better educated due in part to the G.I. Bill,* which assisted veterans transitioning out of the military. In addition to loans and unemployment compensation, the legislation provided aid for vocational training and college. Consequently, a flood of skilled laborers and professionals entered the workforce.

Postwar prosperity enabled the United States to provide aid to foreign countries. The war left much of Europe in ruins. Millions of people were without basic necessities and some were near starvation. President Truman's secretary of state, George C. Marshall, developed a plan to assist nations on the war-ravaged continent, including Germany. The Marshall Plan was remarkably successful. By the end of 1951, most economies in Western Europe were stronger than before the war.

Though not included in the Marshall Plan, Japan also received enormous help in rebuilding its economy and infrastructure. The success there, too, was phenomenal. Germany and Japan became allies of the United States, but tight restrictions placed on both countries kept them incapable of waging war again.

Nazi atrocities against Jews before and during World War II made much of the world sympathetic to the creation of a Jewish state in Palestine, an area along the eastern Mediterranean Sea that includes the city of Jerusalem. For centuries the dispersed Jewish people had longed to gather to that Middle East region regarded by them as their homeland from Biblical times. Arabs already living there were just as convinced that the land was their own ancestral home.

In 1947 the United Nations approved a plan to partition Palestine into two territories, one Jewish and the other Arab. The provisional Jewish government declared independence the following year, and President Truman immediately gave formal U.S. recognition to the new nation of Israel. The first Arab-Israeli war ensued, and hostilities have continued to the present day.

* *"G.I." was an abbreviation originally used by the U.S. Army for "galvanized iron," the material from which many supplies were made. Later, it stood for "government issue," or any article distributed by the military. Finally, it came to mean any member of the United States armed forces.*

60
COMMUNISM and the COLD WAR

The principal ally of the United States in World War II, besides Great Britain, was the U.S.S.R., a communist nation. Under Soviet-style communism, one political party controlled the government and regulated much of the activity in a country. Civil liberties were severely limited, including private property rights.

After the war, the Russians assumed control of eastern Germany, and the other major Allied powers – the U.S., Great Britain, and France – assumed control of the western part. Berlin, the German capital located deep inside Soviet-controlled eastern Germany, was similarly divided into an eastern sector controlled by the Russians and a western sector controlled by the other Allies.

The U.S.S.R. moved to gain control of all of Eastern Europe, which included Poland, Czechoslovakia, Hungary, Romania, and Bulgaria. In those countries, the Russians set up puppet communist governments that took orders from Moscow, the Soviet capital.

Winston Churchill warned in 1946 that an "Iron Curtain" had descended across the European continent. The metaphor described the closing off of Eastern Europe from the democratic capitalist countries of Western Europe. A Cold War had begun. Provocative actions by the communists threatened to escalate into a "hot war" (shooting war) with Western nations.

The U.S. adopted a new foreign policy to contain efforts by the Russians to expand their communist influence. Under the Truman Doctrine, America extended both economic and military aid to free peoples "resisting attempted subjugation by armed minorities or by outside pressures."

A major crisis in the Cold War arose in 1948 when the communists cut off railway, highway, and waterway access into West Berlin, an enclave of democracy and capitalism surrounded by communist East Germany. Avoiding a direct confrontation on the ground, the United States and other Western nations thwarted the blockade with a massive airlift of supplies to the isolated western half of the divided city. The Berlin Airlift continued until the communists backed down the following year and lifted the blockade.

To counter the threat posed by the U.S.S.R. and its Eastern Bloc partners, the United States and 11 other nations formed a security alliance called the North Atlantic Treaty Organization (NATO).

That same year, 1949, President Truman made the sobering announcement that the Russians had carried out a successful test of an atom bomb. The U.S. had remained the sole atomic power for only four years. The Soviet Union and the United States would eventually develop nuclear weapons with a thousand times more destructive power than the atom bombs dropped on Japan, and both nations would build airplanes, submarines, and missiles capable of delivering nuclear strikes anywhere in the world.

The nuclear arms race and the spread of communism would dominate American foreign policy for decades. In the face of these ongoing threats and unlike previous postwar periods, the United States maintained a high level of military readiness to ensure national security, support its allies, and protect American interests around the world.* Private industry worked closely with the military to constantly upgrade weapons systems.

Nuclear technology was not used strictly for weapons. In 1957 America's first commercial nuclear power plant for generating electricity was put into service in western Pennsylvania.

Reports of communist subversives in the U.S. prompted investigations of federal employees and began a period later dubbed the Red Scare. The color red has long been associated with communism. Between 1947 and 1956 the government screened five million federal employees and dismissed 2,700 as security risks; 12,000 resigned.

Alger Hiss, who had held a number of government positions and was suspected of espionage, was convicted of perjury in connection with an investigation of his activities. The case against Julius and Ethel Rosenberg was more alarming. A U.S. district court found them guilty of treason for supplying the Russians with classified information about America's atomic weapons program. The couple was executed in the electric chair in 1953.

The government also investigated the entertainment industry for communist ties. The careers of some prominent figures were damaged or ruined when they became suspects and were blacklisted by the studios.

Senator Joseph McCarthy of Wisconsin gained national attention by claiming that communists had infiltrated the U.S. government. His tactics and decorum during congressional hearings in 1954 led to his being formally condemned by the Senate.

* *The number of active U.S. military troops in 2016 was 1.3 million, with 124,000 based in California, 115,000 in Texas, 39,000 in Hawaii, and 19,000 in Alaska. Of those stationed in foreign countries, 47,000 were in Japan, 35,000 in Germany, 25,000 in South Korea, 12,000 in Italy, 9,000 in the United Kingdom, 6,000 in Kuwait, 4,000 in Bahrain, 3,000 in Qatar, 3,000 in Spain, and 3,000 in Turkey. In addition, more than 800,000 serve in the National Guard and the Reserves.*

61
CHINA and KOREA

After the Second World War, Chinese communists under the leadership of Mao Tse-tung renewed their civil war to overthrow the non-communist, pro-Western Nationalist government in China led by Chiang Kai-shek. The United States did not send troops but otherwise supported the Nationalists. It was not enough. Chiang and the Nationalists were defeated in 1949 and fled to Taiwan (formerly known as Formosa), an island off the Chinese coast. The victorious Mao declared his People's Republic of China (PRC) the legitimate government. In the U.S. it was more common to refer to mainland China as Red China or Communist China.

In the closing days of World War II, the United States and the Soviet Union agreed to divide the Korean peninsula along the 38th parallel, or latitude line. The U.S. took control of the South and supported the creation of a representative government. Russia took control of the North and installed a communist government.*

In 1950 North Korea invaded the South. The United States led a 15-member United Nations coalition to defend South Korea. American general Douglas MacArthur was given command of the U.N. forces.

The communists nearly overran South Korea before the coalition could launch a counteroffensive beginning with an amphibious landing at Inchon. After regaining control of the South, coalition troops pushed far into North Korea near the Chinese border. With U.N. forces poised to win control of the entire peninsula, China sent 300,000 soldiers across the Yalu River into Korea, forcing coalition troops to retreat back into the South.

General MacArthur advocated a strategy for total victory that included the bombing of China to keep supplies and reinforcements from coming down into Korea. Neither President Truman nor the other leaders of the coalition supported such a move that would have risked all-out war with China, Soviet retaliation in Europe, and a nuclear confrontation with the U.S.S.R. The decision was made to maintain a defensive position near the 38th parallel while seeking a negotiated settlement. After MacArthur publicly challenged the president's policy of containment and limited war, Truman relieved MacArthur of command and replaced him with General Matthew Ridgway.

Negotiations to end the fighting began in 1951. A truce signed two years later left Korea divided roughly along the same line as before the war, but relations between the two Koreas have remained hostile. Thirty-seven thousand American servicemen died in the conflict, and 103,000 were wounded.

* *In 1948 the Soviets designated Kim Il-sung as the head of the North Korean government. Upon his death in 1994, he was succeeded by his son, Kim Jong-il, who died in 2011 and was succeeded by his son, Kim Jong-un, the current leader and heir to the communist dynasty.*

62

CIVIL RIGHTS, TELEVISION,
INTERSTATES, and ROCK & ROLL

In the aftermath of the American Civil War, state and local governments, primarily in the South, passed measures to keep blacks and whites separated. At the national level, the Supreme Court in 1896 ruled in *Plessy v. Ferguson* that racial segregation did not necessarily deprive blacks of equal protection of the laws, as guaranteed by the 14th Amendment. Segregation was also practiced in ways not specifically addressed by law. This legal and cultural separation of the races was known as "Jim Crow."

With some exceptions since the Founding, blacks who served in the U.S. military were relegated to segregated units. In 1948 President Truman issued an executive order to begin the integration of the armed services, a goal that was achieved during the Korean War.

Before the 1950s it was common in the United States for black and white children to attend separate public schools. That began to change when Oliver Brown and other African-American parents in Topeka, Kansas, filed suit in federal court against the local school board because of its policy of segregation. The plaintiffs contended that their children were being denied an equal education because black schools were inferior.

The district court sided with the school board. The case, *Brown v. Board of Education*, was appealed to the Supreme Court. In 1954 the High Court reversed the lower court's ruling and found in favor of the plaintiffs, striking down the "separate but equal" doctrine in public education as a violation of the 14th Amendment. This repudiation of the *Plessy* decision paved the way for the integration of black and white children in all public schools.

In 1957 only 20 percent of blacks in the country were registered to vote. President Dwight D. Eisenhower signed a civil rights bill that year to strengthen African-American voting rights, which had been suppressed for decades in parts of the South through poll taxes, literacy tests, and intimidation.*

A new form of mass communication came to prominence in the 1950s. An American farm boy, Philo T. Farnsworth, conceived the basic elements of the technology back in the 1920s. Television was ready to be marketed when World War II broke out, but production had to be postponed due to wartime restrictions on non-military manufacturing. After the war, television grew into a major industry. The first TV sets had small screens, the picture was in black and white, and programming was very limited, but by 1955 two-thirds of American households owned a TV.

In aviation, the advances made during World War II were put to civilian use. Passenger planes after the war flew farther, faster, and higher. Electronic equipment helped pilots avoid dangerous weather. Airplanes replaced trains and ocean liners as the preferred mode of mass transportation over long distances. In 1958 the first American commercial jet airliner, the Boeing 707, went into service.

Construction of an interstate road system got underway in the 1950s. President Eisenhower championed the ambitious plan. These multi-lane divided highways, free of stop signs and traffic lights, made it possible to travel from Florida to Michigan on just one road, Interstate 75 (I-75). Interstate 80 stretched all the way from New Jersey to California. The 47,000 miles of interstate highways changed the face of America and have had a profound impact on the economy.

In music, the Big Bands of the 1930s and '40s gave way to a new genre in the '50s called rock and roll. Elvis Presley was recognized as the "King" of the new music. The main instruments used – guitar, bass, keyboard, and drums – enabled the musicians to double as singers.

After many decades as U.S. territories, Alaska and Hawaii became the 49th and 50th states, respectively, in 1959. With statehood came representation in Congress and the right of residents to vote in congressional and presidential elections. For the first time since 1912, stars had to be added to the American flag to reflect the current number of states. Alaska and Hawaii are the only non-contiguous states in the nation.

* *According to the U.S. Census Bureau, 73 percent of blacks were registered to vote in 2012 and 66 percent voted. Seventy-two percent of whites were registered and 62 percent voted. Ninety-three million eligible voters did not go to the polls.*

63
SPUTNIK, CASTRO, and KENNEDY

In 1957 the Soviet Union shocked the world, especially the U.S., by launching the first satellite into space. Satellites are unmanned spacecraft used for the collection of scientific data and for communications, weather forecasting, and military surveillance. The Soviets called their satellite *Sputnik*. Its orbital path took it over the United States. The

U.S. put its first satellite into orbit the following year. Along with the arms race, America and the U.S.S.R. were now competitors in a space race.

In 1960 relations between the two superpowers were strained further when the Soviets shot down an American U-2 spy plane flying high over Russia and captured the pilot. After first claiming that the plane had been conducting weather research, the Eisenhower administration acknowledged that its mission was part of the extensive aerial reconnaissance conducted covertly by the United States to guard against a surprise attack like Pearl Harbor.

Communism spread in the Western Hemisphere in the 1950s. The most alarming instance was in Cuba. When Fidel Castro overthrew the dictator of that island in 1959, most Americans initially viewed it as a positive development, but Castro turned out to be a communist who confiscated property and ruled as a dictator himself. The United States imposed an economic embargo against Cuba in 1960 and severed diplomatic relations the following year when that island nation, only 90 miles off the southern coast of Florida, aligned itself with the Soviet Union.

In the presidential election of 1960, Richard Nixon, vice-president in the Eisenhower administration, was the Republican nominee and John F. Kennedy, the junior senator from Massachusetts, was the Democratic nominee. The candidates began a tradition in presidential races of facing the nation in live televised debates. Kennedy's victory at age 43 made him the youngest president ever elected.

64
SUPERPOWER STANDOFF

Soon after his inauguration, President Kennedy signed an executive order creating the Peace Corps. This federal agency recruits American volunteers to work for two years improving the lives of people around the world. Members of the Peace Corps provide assistance in agriculture, education, business and community development, and the environment.*

In April of 1961 Kennedy authorized an invasion of Cuba to overthrow the communist dictatorship of Fidel Castro with help from opposition groups on the island. The U.S. Central Intelligence Agency (CIA), which orchestrated the plan, hoped to obscure American involvement by recruiting 1,500 Cuban exiles living in Miami, Florida, to carry out the operation. Support planes used in the attack were painted in the colors of the Cuban air force to add to the deception.

The amphibious landing took place on the southern coast of Cuba at the Bay of Pigs. President Kennedy canceled vital air support after the assault was already underway. The mission failed after three days. Of the CIA operatives involved in the action, 100 were killed and 1,200 were taken prisoner.[†] The Castro regime executed hundreds of dissident Cuban citizens in the subsequent crackdown.

In Europe, so many citizens were fleeing the oppression and deprivation in East Germany that it was having a serious negative effect on that communist country's economy and political standing in the world. To stem the flow of escapees, East Germany, with support from the Soviet Union, began constructing a wall around democratic West Berlin in August of 1961. This heightened tensions because it was not known if the communists intended to block access to West Berlin, as they had done in 1948. But there was a bigger concern. If the wall had been a precursor to an attempted takeover, the United States might have had to use its tactical nuclear weapons to defend the city.

President Kennedy dispatched his vice-president to West Berlin. In a show of force, he also sent 1,500 American soldiers to reinforce the Allied military units already there. After traveling in a large convoy over one of the highway access routes through East Germany, the troops were allowed to pass through communist checkpoints and enter West Berlin. The city remained free and its access to the outside world remained open, but construction of the wall continued and the communists severed rail lines into West Berlin so East Germans could not escape to freedom. The Berlin Wall would stand as a symbol of the Cold War for decades.

A more serious threat arose the following year. Photographs taken by U.S. satellites and spy planes in 1962 revealed the existence of Soviet missiles in Cuba. The missiles, which could be armed with nuclear warheads, were capable of hitting American cities within minutes. President Kennedy considered using air strikes or a full military invasion to destroy the missile sites, but he opted for a blockade of Cuba using the U.S. Navy, the Coast Guard, and the Air Force to prevent the Soviets from supplying additional offensive weapons.

Not knowing how the Russians would respond, America prepared for nuclear war with its Cold War adversary. By this time, the United States and the U.S.S.R. possessed enough weapons to destroy the major cities of both countries in a full-scale nuclear exchange. After several tense days under the threat, the Soviets agreed to remove their missile installations from Cuba in return for a U.S. pledge to remove its missiles from Turkey, a country bordering the Soviet Union.

* *The Peace Corps has sent 220,000 volunteers to 140 countries since its inception.*

† *Castro released the captured Cuban exiles to the United States in 1962 in exchange for $3 million in cash and $53 million worth of medical supplies and other goods raised from private donations.*

65
ASSASSINATION and the GREAT SOCIETY

On November 22, 1963, President Kennedy was visiting Texas to shore up support for his reelection. As he rode through downtown Dallas waving to crowds from an open limousine, he was shot by an unseen gunman. The Secret Service, responsible for protecting the president, rushed him to a hospital where he was pronounced dead.* Local police arrested Lee Harvey Oswald for the shooting less than an hour later.

Vice-President Lyndon Johnson, who had been riding in the motorcade two cars behind Kennedy, was sworn in as president aboard Air Force One that afternoon, before the presidential plane took off for the return flight to Washington, D.C. First Lady Jacqueline Kennedy, who had been sitting next to her husband when he was shot, rode in the rear of the plane with the casket.

Two days later, as Oswald was being transferred to a different Dallas jail, a man stepped out from a crowd of onlookers and fatally shot him. Police quickly subdued and arrested the assailant.

Johnson won the 1964 presidential election in a landslide. He pushed through legislation that provided extensive and sustained federal funding to wage a "war on poverty" and bring about a "Great Society" in America.

The government established the Head Start program to help disadvantaged children of pre-school age and appropriated money for education at the elementary, secondary, and college levels. Job training was provided and loans to small businesses were made available. The government created the National Endowment for the Arts, the National Endowment for the Humanities, the Corporation for Public Broadcasting, and two new cabinet-level agencies: the Department of Housing & Urban Development (HUD) and the Department of Transportation (DOT).

Medicare was instituted to subsidize the medical care of Americans age 65 and older. Medicaid subsidized the medical care of low-income families and individuals under 65.[†] The poor also became eligible for food stamps that could be used in lieu of money to purchase groceries.[‡] With these programs and others, the number of Americans receiving direct financial assistance from the government rose considerably.

In 1965 a new immigration law abolished the national origins formula created in the 1920s and gave foreigners of every nationality an equal opportunity to become U.S. citizens. The legislation also marked the first time that reuniting families was given priority over the job skills of applicants. Annual ceilings were set for each hemisphere: 170,000 for the Eastern and 120,000 for the Western. The limits did not apply, however, to foreigners with immediate family members who were already American citizens or permanent resident aliens. As a result, the number of immigrant visas issued far exceeded the limits.[§]

* *Assassins killed two other presidents besides Kennedy and Lincoln: James Garfield in 1881 and William McKinley in 1901.*

† *Medicare and Medicaid together currently account for 27% of the federal budget.*

‡ *Food stamp statistics from the U.S. Department of Agriculture:*

	Recipients	Households	% of Pop	Expenditures
1990	20M	8M	8%	15B
2000	17M	7M	6%	17B
2010	40M	19M	13%	68B
2015	46M	23M	14%	74B

§ *Immigration surged to more than 800,000 per year by the 1990s, and the main countries of origin shifted from Europe to Latin America and Asia. According to the U.S. Census Bureau:*

Foreign-born Population		
	1960	2014
in millions	10	42
% tot pop	5%	13%

Foreign-born Population by Region of Origin		
	1960	2014
Europe	75%	11%
Canada	10%	2%
Latin America	9%	52%
Asia	5%	30%
Other	1%	5%

66
I HAVE A DREAM

In 1963 the civil rights leader and minister, Dr. Martin Luther King Jr., led 250,000 people in a march on Washington, D.C. The event culminated with his visionary speech from the steps of the Lincoln Memorial. He told the crowd:

> I have a dream that one day this nation will rise up and live out the true meaning of its creed: We hold these truths to be self-evident, that all men are created equal. I have a dream that my four little children will one day live in a nation where they will not be judged by the color of their skin but by the content of their character.

Before 1964 it was common in the South to find restaurants, hotels, theaters, restrooms, drinking fountains, and swimming pools designated "whites only." Where admittance was open to all, blacks were often restricted to certain areas such as the back of the bus or the balcony of the theater. A civil rights bill enacted that year outlawed discrimination in public places, employment, and public schools on the basis of race, color, religion, sex, or national origin.

In metropolitan areas, a demographic shift that began in the 1940s continued into the 1960s as large numbers of families moved to the suburbs, leaving inner cities with predominantly minority populations and a diminished tax base. To achieve racial desegregation in public schools, some students were bused to schools outside the neighborhoods where they lived.

Racial tensions sparked 750 riots during the '60s. In 1965 six days of rioting in the Los Angeles neighborhood of Watts left 34 people dead, a thousand injured, and 800 buildings damaged or destroyed. Forty-three people died in the Detroit riots of 1967, and 2,000 buildings were burned. Soldiers had to be mobilized to help police restore order. The worst year for riots was 1968, the year a gunman assassinated Martin Luther King in Memphis, Tennessee.

In the midst of the unrest, a milestone was reached when Thurgood Marshall, previously chief counsel for the National Association for the Advancement of Colored People (NAACP), became the first African-American Supreme Court justice.

67
VIETNAM

The Geneva Conference of 1954 partitioned the French colony of Vietnam much like Korea, with a communist government in the North and a pro-Western, non-communist government in the South. The

United States supported the South Vietnamese with military advisors and weapons because President Eisenhower believed a communist takeover there would have a domino effect and lead to other countries in the region falling to communism. President Kennedy increased U.S. troop levels in Vietnam to 16,000 in 1963.

The following year, three North Vietnamese torpedo boats fired on an American destroyer conducting reconnaissance in international waters in the Gulf of Tonkin. The destroyer returned fire and called in air support. All three North Vietnamese vessels sustained damage but returned to their base. The U.S. ship and its support aircraft were unscathed. This minor naval engagement and an erroneous report of a second attack two days later were the incidents that precipitated a massive and protracted commitment of the armed forces of the United States.

President Johnson ordered retaliatory air strikes against North Vietnam. Without declaring war, Congress authorized the president to conduct military operations in Southeast Asia. As the U.S. assumed the primary role in South Vietnam's defense, Johnson drastically increased American troop strength in the region to 500,000 by 1968. The North Vietnamese received support from their communist allies, China and the Soviet Union.

Televised news reports showing the death and destruction in Vietnam eroded support for the war and President Johnson. In an unusual move for an incumbent, he decided not to seek reelection.

In the 1968 presidential race, the country elected Richard Nixon in his second bid for the White House. After he took office, President Nixon began withdrawing American troops from Vietnam, and South Vietnamese forces took on an ever-increasing role. The process was called Vietnamization. Bombing by U.S. aircraft intensified, however, and covert military operations were carried out in Laos and Cambodia to block communist supply lines.

Opposition to the war continued. Music by the Beatles, Bob Dylan, and other popular artists were vehicles for protest. Demonstrations sprang up across the United States, particularly on college campuses. At Kent State University in Ohio, National Guard troops trying to control a crowd shot and killed four students.

Hundreds of thousands of young men evaded the draft; 90,000 moved to Canada. In 1972 the U.S. discontinued conscription, and military service became voluntary.*

The United States and South Vietnam signed peace accords with North Vietnam the following year, and America withdrew the last of its troops. What President Nixon called "peace with honor" was a stalemate more shaky than the one in Korea. Just two years later, in 1975, the North Vietnamese conquered the South and united both Vietnams under communist rule.

More than three million U.S. troops served in Southeast Asia over the course of the war. Fifty-eight thousand were killed and 300,000 were wounded. Unlike their counterparts in previous wars, those who made it back home from Vietnam did not return to public celebrations in their honor, and some faced ridicule for having served.

* *Nearly all male citizens ages 18 through 25 are still required by law to register with Selective Service, the federal agency that administers the draft when it is in effect. Although women have never been subject to the draft, more than two million have voluntarily enlisted in the U.S. military over the years. The 210,000 women serving in the armed forces in 2016 represented 16 percent of total active duty personnel.*

68
FEMINISM, DRUGS, and the ENVIRONMENT

Race relations and Vietnam were not the only issues fueling the political and social upheaval of the 1960s; feminism was another. That movement addressed the role of women in society and pushed for an end to sex discrimination. Employment was a chief concern. Women objected to being paid less than men for doing the same work, and they sought equal opportunity for jobs often regarded as "man's work." Women wanted to remove the "glass ceiling" that kept them from attaining the top positions in organizations. Abortion also became a central issue, especially after a 1973 Supreme Court decision, *Roe v. Wade*, made the procedure legal throughout the country.

The abuse of legal drugs increased in the Sixties, as did the use of illegal substances such as marijuana, cocaine, and the hallucinogen LSD. Cohabitation and sexual relations between unmarried individuals began to lose much of the stigma that had existed previously.

The environment was a prominent issue for the government and the general public. Studies revealed alarming levels of pollution in the air, water, and soil. Environmentalists raised concerns over the destruction of forests and wetlands and the possible extinction of certain species, including the Bald Eagle, a national symbol. President Nixon signed legislation to punish polluters and protect the environment and threatened wildlife. Public and private efforts to recycle newspapers and containers made from metal, plastic, and glass gained momentum.

69
ONE GIANT LEAP FOR MANKIND

The Soviet Union was the early leader in space exploration. The first satellite and the first manned spacecraft to orbit the Earth were Russian. The first manned U.S. rocket, launched in 1961 from Cape Canaveral, Florida, carried astronaut Alan Shepard 100 miles out over the Atlantic Ocean in a 15-minute suborbital flight. It was a minor achievement compared to what the Soviets had done, but just three weeks later President Kennedy laid out his vision for America's fledgling space program and set a goal to land a man on the moon and return him safely to the Earth before the end of the decade. The National Aeronautics and Space Administration (NASA) accepted the bold challenge.

The first American in orbit was John Glenn, who circled the Earth three times during a five-hour flight in 1962. Subsequent flights by other astronauts included many orbits over several days. In addition to manned space missions, the United States launched numerous satellites into orbit and sent probes to explore the solar system.

On July 20, 1969, two U.S. astronauts landed their Apollo 11 spacecraft on the moon. People all over the world watched on live television as the mission commander, Neil Armstrong, stepped down onto the powdery lunar surface and said, "That's one small step for [a] man, one giant leap for mankind." The astronauts transmitted back spectacular pictures of the blue Earth suspended in the blackness of space. NASA successfully completed five more manned lunar missions over the next three years.

70
CHINA and RUSSIA, WATERGATE, and OIL

Richard Nixon built a reputation as a staunch anti-communist over many years in elective office. So it came as a surprise when, in his first term as president, he reached out to America's two biggest rivals, both communist nations. Nixon reversed two decades of U.S. policy by officially recognizing the People's Republic of China and supporting its admission to the U.N. In 1972 he became the first president to visit China. Later that year he visited Moscow, another first for a U.S. president. While there, Nixon and the Soviet leader signed an agreement that placed limits on the nuclear arsenals of both superpowers.

On the heels of these momentous events, President Nixon's reelection was widely expected. Nevertheless, members of his administration and campaign committee hired operatives to break into the headquarters of the Democratic Party to photograph confidential documents and plant electronic eavesdropping devices. The offices were located in the Watergate building in Washington, D.C. Police caught the burglars in the act. Nixon denied any involvement and easily won reelection, carrying all but one state.

In October 1973 war broke out in the Middle East. In an attempt to regain territory lost in a previous conflict, Egypt and Syria unleashed surprise attacks on Israel during Yom Kippur, one of the holiest days of the year for Jews. After two days of setbacks, the Israeli military rallied and stopped the Arab advance, but with supplies running low, Israel appealed for help. In the face of Arab and Soviet threats against any nation that came to Israel's aid, President Nixon ordered an enormous airlift of military equipment and supplies. The Israelis went on the offensive, took back territory lost in the initial stages, and had the Egyptian army trapped when a negotiated ceasefire went into effect.

The Organization of Petroleum Exporting Countries (OPEC), composed largely of Arab nations, retaliated against the U.S. by imposing an oil embargo. The spike in fuel prices contributed to an economic slump. The energy crisis in America resulted in long lines at gas stations and an emphasis on conservation and domestic oil exploration.

President Nixon signed legislation authorizing the construction of an 800-mile pipeline in Alaska to carry crude oil from the large oil field at Prudhoe Bay in the north to the Port of Valdez in the south. From there, the raw material could be loaded onto tanker ships and transported to refineries in the lower 48 states. To promote fuel conservation, the federal government mandated a maximum speed limit of 55 miles per hour for the nation's highways.

71
RESIGNATION and HOSTAGES

From the beginning of President Nixon's second term, mounting evidence suggested that, contrary to White House assertions, members of the president's administration, his campaign committee, and the president himself were involved in the Watergate affair. During congressional hearings convened to investigate the matter, a White House aide revealed that Nixon had made audio recordings of Oval Office meetings. Congress subpoenaed the tapes, which provided evidence that the president had abused his authority. While he did not order the Watergate break-in, he tried to cover up the involvement of others after the fact, which is a crime.

Before articles of impeachment could be brought to the floor of the House of Representatives in 1974, Nixon resigned. He was the only president in history to do so. The vice-president, Gerald Ford, was sworn in as president immediately following Nixon's departure from the White House. Ford believed it was not in the country's best interest for a former president to be pursued in the courts. Exercising his constitutional prerogative, President Ford granted Nixon a full and unconditional pardon for any crimes he committed while in office. Other members of Nixon's administration and campaign organization were tried, convicted, and sent to prison.

Jimmy Carter, who had served as Georgia's governor, beat Ford in the 1976 presidential campaign. Carter brought the leaders of Egypt and Israel together to negotiate an historic peace accord. It was a remarkable achievement given the fact that the two countries had fought each other five times in the previous 28 years, but two foreign policy setbacks in 1979 eclipsed that success.

The first incident occurred when Iranians stormed the U.S. embassy in the capital city of Tehran and took 52 Americans hostage. Negotiations failed to win their release, and a rescue attempt by the United States military had to be aborted in the Iranian desert because of equipment malfunctions. The second major challenge came when the Soviet Union invaded Afghanistan and installed a communist government in that country.

Domestic problems in the U.S., particularly with the economy, compounded President Carter's difficulties. Inflation nearly tripled during his term of office. Inflation is a rise in the price of goods and services relative to the money supply. Money decreases in value.

High interest rates were another impediment to economic growth. Most individuals and families borrow money to purchase houses, cars, and other high-dollar items. Businesses take out loans to buy inventory and equipment. A high rate of interest makes borrowing more difficult and costly. With money harder to come by, consumers and businesses do not buy as much, and the economy suffers.

In the presidential election of 1980, President Carter lost in a landslide to Ronald Reagan, a former governor of California, a movie and TV actor, and the oldest president ever elected. On the day the 69-year-old Reagan was inaugurated, Iran released all the American hostages it had held for 444 days.

REAGAN REVOLUTION

A central theme of President Reagan's political philosophy was expressed in his statement, "Government is too big, and it spends too much." His plan called for cuts in federal programs and regulations, reductions in the number of government employees, and tax reform that included increased incentives for business investment and dramatically lower income tax rates.* He pushed for increased military spending, though, because he regarded the Soviet Union as an "evil empire" bent on world domination.

Reagan's approach to communist expansion was a departure from the containment policies of previous presidents. Using overt and covert means, he sought to roll back gains the communists had already made. The new strategy was implemented in Eastern Europe, Latin America, Africa, Cambodia, and Afghanistan.

Two months after taking office in 1981, President Reagan narrowly survived an assassination attempt. He made a full recovery from the gunshot wound and later that year appointed the first female justice to the Supreme Court: Sandra Day O'Connor.

Reagan's policies triggered an unprecedented economic expansion that created millions of jobs. Federal revenue increased, but federal spending increased even more, and the national debt rose significantly.† Deficit spending is made possible with money the federal government borrows from state and local governments, from foreign governments, from individual and corporate investors in the United States and abroad, and from the federal government's own trust funds, such as the Social Security Trust Fund.

During his second term President Reagan authorized the covert sale of weapons to Iran to forge a relationship with what were believed to be moderate elements within that country, which was governed by a militant Islamic theocracy. Reagan hoped the overture would thwart Soviet diplomatic efforts in Iran and lead to the release of American hostages being held in Lebanon by pro-Iranian terrorists. The transactions were an exception to the embargo on weapons sales to Iran and ran counter to U.S. policy against bargaining with terrorists.

Profits from the sales were funneled to Contra rebels fighting to topple the communist Sandinista government in Nicaragua. This circumvented legislation that prohibited the United States from giving aid to the Contras. After a number of investigations, some members of the Reagan administration were indicted and convicted. The president denied any knowledge of the diversion of funds and was not charged with a crime.

Increases in U.S. military spending, the deployment of nuclear missiles in Europe, and President Reagan's insistence on pursuing the Strategic Defense Initiative (SDI) pressured the Kremlin to negotiate an end to the arms race. The goal of SDI was to build a virtual shield against nuclear missile attacks using ground-based and space-based sensors and interceptors. Although the program was only in the planning stage, SDI played a key role in bringing the United States and the Soviet Union together to reduce, not just limit, the quantity of nuclear weapons on both sides.

After two terms as vice-president in the Reagan administration, George H.W. Bush was elected president in 1988. During his presidency, communist rule in Eastern Europe and the Soviet Union collapsed. For 44 years the U.S.S.R. had dominated Eastern Europe. Then, beginning in 1989, popular uprisings led to free elections. First in Poland, then in Czechoslovakia,‡ Hungary, Bulgaria, and Romania, the control of the communist party came to an end. Unlike his predecessors, the new leader of the Soviet Union, Mikhail Gorbachev, did not take action to crush the revolts.

In Germany, citizens began tearing down the Berlin Wall, a symbol of the Cold War since 1961. In 1990 Berlin became one city again and East Germany and West Germany merged to form a reunified and democratic Germany after 45 years of division.

Finally, the Soviet Union itself broke apart. Since 1922 it had been a nation of republics under the control of the communist party and the Soviet leadership in Moscow. Following the lead of Eastern Europe, the republics began rejecting communism and, one by one, declared independence. By the end of 1991 the U.S.S.R. no longer existed; in its place were 15 separate non-communist nations.

The Cold War – that struggle between East and West, between Soviet-backed communism and democracy and free enterprise, which had kept the world under the specter of nuclear war for decades – was over.

---

* *Under President Reagan, the top marginal income tax rate for individuals was lowered from 70 percent to 28 percent. The highest corporate income tax rate went from 46 percent to 34 percent.*

† *The national debt grew from $908 billion in 1980 to $2.6 trillion in 1988. In 2016 the debt exceeded $19 trillion, more than the gross domestic product (GDP), the value of the nation's entire annual output of goods and services.*

‡ *In 1993 the people of Czechoslovakia peacefully divided their country into two sovereign states: the Czech Republic and Slovakia.*

73
GULF WAR, CLINTON, and the DIGITAL AGE

Iraq's invasion of Kuwait in 1990 threw the Middle East into crisis and threatened to disrupt the flow of oil through the Persian Gulf, a vital trade route for the world economy. The U.S. assembled a coalition of 34 nations to remove the Iraqis. The Gulf War began in January 1991 with a massive air campaign. The following month ground troops took just four days to liberate Kuwait and force Iraq's capitulation.

After the Gulf War the U.S. economy went into recession. While a recession is less severe than a depression, two million Americans lost their jobs as companies cut costs. President Bush's popularity quickly evaporated in the wake of persistent bad news about the economy. Arkansas Governor Bill Clinton defeated Bush in the 1992 election.

The economy rebounded during the Clinton years. The North American Free Trade Agreement (NAFTA) and the General Agreement on Tariffs and Trade (GATT) lowered or removed barriers to foreign trade. The stock market rallied as more Americans than ever before acquired a stake in financial markets through personal investment accounts and 401(k) employee retirement plans. Investors poured billions of dollars into computer-related companies. The internet was heralded as the basis for a new economy and the centerpiece of a new period in human progress: the Information Age. The period was also dubbed the Digital Age as microchips and computers found their way into practically every business and home. Steve Jobs's company, Apple, and Bill Gates's company, Microsoft, were key players in the proliferation of personal computers.

During President Clinton's second term he was accused of perjury and obstruction of justice in connection with a sexual harassment lawsuit brought against him. In 1998, for only the second time in U.S. history, the House of Representatives impeached the president. The Senate, though, voted well short of the required two-thirds to convict him, and Clinton remained in office.

74
ELECTIONS and ELECTORS

Federal elections are held in the fall of every even year, on the first Tuesday after the first Monday in November. That day was chosen as

Election Day to facilitate voting in an earlier time when the country was largely agrarian. November came after the fall harvest and before winter storms impeded travel over unimproved roads. State and local elections are held at the same time.

Almost all citizens who are 18 and older may register to vote. In the registration process, voters identify themselves as either Republican or Democrat, or a voter may register as an independent, unaffiliated with either party. Political parties have different goals for America and different ideas about the size and role of government. Elections are contests between political parties as well as candidates. Party candidates who win the presidency or a majority of seats in the Senate or House of Representatives give their party more power to enact its platform.

With the exception of independent candidates, citizens who seek elective office must first win the nomination of their party by defeating fellow party candidates vying for the same governmental office. These intra-party political battles are fought in preliminary elections, or primaries, sponsored separately by the Democratic Party and the Republican Party.

Voter eligibility varies depending on the primary. If a particular local or state primary is closed, only party members are allowed to vote. In a semi-closed primary, independent voters are allowed into the process. In an open primary, party members, independents, and members of the opposing party are all allowed to cast ballots. In the primaries as well as the general election, citizens vote in person at their assigned local precinct polling stations, or they may send in absentee ballots through the mail.

To become a party's nominee for a seat in the House of Representatives, a candidate has to win the primary only in his or her own congressional district. A candidate for the U.S. Senate must win a statewide primary.

To clinch a party's presidential nomination, a candidate must compete in primaries or caucuses (a less formal method of voting) in all the states.* The candidate who receives the most votes in these state contests usually becomes the party's nominee. The official nomination takes place at the party's national convention, held in the summer of the election year and attended by delegates from every state and territory. Before or during the convention, the presumptive presidential nominee chooses a running mate to be the nominee for vice-president.

On Election Day in November, the general election, voters choose between the Democrat nominee, the Republican nominee, and the occasional independent candidate to decide who will win each contested office.† Those elected as president, senator, or representative take their oaths of office[‡] and begin serving two months later, in January, to allow time for a smooth transition with outgoing office holders.

The presidential election in the year 2000 was one of the most controversial in history and renewed debate about the process. As stipulated by Article II of the Constitution, the president is not chosen directly by the votes of the people (the popular vote) but by electors.[§]

Each state is allotted a number of electors equal to that state's representation in Congress. For example, a state with 10 seats in the House of Representatives has 12 electors, one for each House member and one for each of the state's two senators. The number of electors in the entire country is equal to the total number of senators (100), plus the total number of congressmen in the House (435), plus three electors from Washington, D.C. The 538 electors, chosen anew with each presidential election, are known collectively as the Electoral College.

On Election Day the presidential nominee who wins the popular vote in a state wins all the electors in that state.[¶] The nominee who receives a majority of the 538 total electoral votes, or at least 270, wins the presidency.

The Electoral College never meets as one body. Electors cast their votes in their respective state houses after the general election. The results are sent to Washington, where Congress tabulates the electoral votes from all the states and formally names the president-elect.

This electoral system is in harmony with the principles of federalism and state representation established by the Framers. It encourages presidential nominees to seek support over a broader area of the country, but it has, on a few occasions, resulted in a president being elected who did not receive a majority of votes cast by citizens in the nation as a whole.[‖] This occurred in the 2000 election, but the main controversy in that race was the vote counting in Florida and the number of ballots that could not be counted for either presidential candidate because they had not been cast properly.

The tally of valid Florida ballots gave the Republican nominee, Texas governor George W. Bush, a slight lead over Al Gore, the Democratic nominee and vice-president in the Clinton administration. Gore did not concede, however, and called for the ballots to be counted again. Legal challenges continued for several weeks until the U.S. Supreme Court halted the recounts. The Florida legislature certified the final tabulation of votes, which showed Bush as the winner. The Florida electors won by Bush put him over the 270 electoral votes needed to win the presidency.

George W. Bush was inaugurated as the 43rd president of the United States in January 2001. His father had been the 41st president. It was only the second time in American history that the child of a president had become president himself. The other father-son presidents were John Adams (the 2nd) and John Quincy Adams (the 6th). Benjamin Harrison, the 23rd president, was the grandson of the 9th president, William Henry Harrison.

* *Since the 1970s, the Iowa caucuses have been the first battleground in the presidential nominating process.*

† *Louisiana, Washington, and California use a top-two system for congressional races. All candidates for a congressional seat, regardless of party affiliation, appear on the same ballot, and all registered voters are eligible to vote. The candidate who receives a majority of votes is elected to the office. If no candidate receives a majority, the two candidates who received the most votes face each other in a runoff election to determine who will win the seat. They can be members of the same party.*

‡ *Article II of the Constitution requires the president to take the following oath: "I do solemnly swear (or affirm) that I will faithfully execute the Office of President of the United States, and will to the best of my ability, preserve, protect and defend the Constitution of the United States." The words "So help me God" are usually added at the end. The Constitution also requires senators, representatives, and executive and judicial officers at the federal and state level to be bound by oath to support the Constitution. Members of the armed forces take an oath to defend the Constitution.*

Though not mandated by the Constitution, new immigrants must take the following oath to become citizens: "I hereby declare, on oath, that I absolutely and entirely renounce and abjure all allegiance and fidelity to any foreign prince, potentate, state, or sovereignty, of whom or which I have heretofore been a subject or citizen; that I will support and defend the Constitution and laws of the United States of America against all enemies, foreign and domestic; that I will bear true faith and allegiance to the same; that I will bear arms on behalf of the United States when required by the law; that I will perform non-combatant service in the Armed Forces of the United States when required by the law; that I will perform work of national importance under civilian direction when required by the law; and that I take this obligation freely, without any mental reservation or purpose of evasion; so help me God."

While facing the American flag, citizens recite the following Pledge of Allegiance in a variety of settings, including in schools and at government and civic meetings:

"I pledge allegiance to the flag of the United States of America,
and to the republic for which it stands, one nation under God,
indivisible, with liberty and justice for all."

§ *The Constitution prohibits members of Congress or anyone else holding federal office from becoming an elector, but otherwise leaves it up to each state to determine how its electors are chosen every four years. Presidential electors are selected by state political parties either in primaries, party conventions, or party committees.*

¶ *Maine and Nebraska are exceptions to the winner-take-all norm. They are the only states where electoral votes can be allocated among presidential candidates.*

‖ *Three presidents elected in the 19th century did not win the nationwide popular vote: John Quincy Adams in 1824, Rutherford B. Hayes in 1876, and Benjamin Harrison in 1888.*

75

9/11 and the WAR ON TERROR

On the morning of September 11, 2001, nineteen suicidal terrorists hijacked four American airliners. They flew two of the planes into the twin towers of the World Trade Center in New York City and crashed a third plane into the Pentagon, the headquarters of the Defense Department in Washington, D.C. The fourth airliner was believed to be heading for the White House or the Capitol building when it went down in a Pennsylvania field as passengers fought the terrorists for control of the plane. The coordinated operation killed nearly 3,000 Americans, including more than 400 firemen, policemen, and paramedics trying to rescue victims at the World Trade Center when the gigantic skyscrapers collapsed.

President Bush vowed to find out who was behind the attacks and bring them to justice. He laid out a comprehensive plan for fighting terrorism globally. The U.S. would enlist the help of other countries in a new kind of war to be waged against terrorists and any government or organization providing support to them.

Airport officials tightened security. A new cabinet-level federal agency, the Department of Homeland Security, was created. State and local governments prepared for and worked to prevent terrorist attacks at their respective levels. American citizens at home and abroad were asked to report suspicious activity and warned to be aware of possible threats.

U.S. intelligence agencies soon discovered that the 9/11 hijackers were members of a worldwide Islamic terrorist organization known as Al-Qaeda and led by Osama bin Laden. The Taliban government in Afghanistan supported bin Laden's activities and had allowed him to set up his headquarters there.

Less than a month after 9/11, the U.S. and Britain, along with some 30 other nations, invaded Afghanistan. The military coalition drove the Taliban regime from power and destroyed the main Al-Qaeda camps, but elements of both organizations remained in the country and bin Laden evaded capture. In spite of the ongoing war, Afghans held elections, and a new representative government began the process of rebuilding the country with support from coalition nations.

The Bush administration regarded Iraq as the next most dangerous threat in the war on terror. The country was a haven for terrorists and a sponsor of terrorist acts, though not implicated in the 9/11 attacks.

The formal ceasefire in the 1991 Gulf War had gone into effect only after Iraq agreed to restrictions to its military capability. For years,

Iraq's president, Saddam Hussein, had thwarted United Nations inspectors trying to verify his government's compliance. He was thought to possess or to be in the process of acquiring chemical, biological, or nuclear weapons, commonly referred to as weapons of mass destruction (WMD).

After Iraq failed to respond fully to diplomatic efforts to resolve the impasse, the United States, with help from the United Kingdom and other nations, invaded Iraq in 2003. With amazing speed, coalition forces defeated the Iraqi military and toppled the government but did not find weapons of mass destruction.

Most Iraqis welcomed the downfall of the brutal Hussein regime. Securing the peace proved to be much more difficult. Terrorists from other countries joined Iraqi insurgents in disrupting and killing military personnel and Iraqi citizens trying to establish a free society after decades under a dictatorship.

Despite the instability caused by the lack of security, the Iraqi people ratified a constitution and elected representatives to a new government. They created a tribunal to bring members of the old guard to justice for their crimes. Saddam Hussein was hanged after a lengthy trial.

76
FINANCIAL CRISIS

Low interest rates, relaxed qualifications for home loans, and rapidly appreciating real estate values contributed to a boom in construction, home sales, and financing beginning around 1998. But borrowers took on too much debt, including loans for cash using the appreciated equity in their homes as collateral. Banks and other lenders, in some instances under pressure from federal agencies and community organizations, made "subprime" loans to home buyers whose credit worthiness did not meet conventional standards. Investment bankers bought the subprime mortgage receivables from lenders, packaged them into various pools to spread the risk, and used them as collateral for securities sold in financial markets.

Rampant speculation contributed to the housing boom. In 2005, 28 percent of the homes sold were bought as investment properties, and 12 percent were for vacation homes. Primary residences accounted for only 60 percent of purchases, a record low.

In 2006 the housing market cooled. A large and growing inventory of unsold properties caused home values to fall. Homeowners with subprime loans who could not afford the monthly payments, and real estate investors who could not pay multiple mortgages for a prolonged length of time were unable to sell their properties or refinance their loans. The value of millions of homes dropped below what was owed on them.

As borrowers defaulted in large numbers, banks and other firms with substantial holdings in "toxic" mortgage-related assets incurred huge losses, scaled back their lending, and saw precipitous drops in their stock prices and cash reserves.

With the country sliding into a recession brought on by the housing and mortgage meltdown, the federal government intervened to stimulate the economy and bail out certain financial institutions and other businesses deemed too large to fail.

The Federal National Mortgage Association (commonly known as Fannie Mae) and the Federal Home Loan Mortgage Corporation (commonly known as Freddie Mac) were government-sponsored enterprises created decades earlier to promote and facilitate home ownership through lending. These two publicly traded corporations owned or guaranteed half of the $12 trillion in mortgages in the United States, but they were buckling under the weight of bad subprime mortgages they had taken on. Worried that bankruptcies of that magnitude might cripple the nation's financial system, the federal government took over the two corporations in September 2008.

The largest bankruptcy in history occurred that same month when the Wall Street financial services firm of Lehman Brothers went under due to its stake in subprime mortgages. This was followed by the collapse of Washington Mutual, the largest U.S. bank failure ever.

In October, President Bush signed legislation that created the Troubled Asset Relief Program (TARP). The bill gave the Treasury secretary broad authority to spend $700 billion to rescue the faltering economy. The secretary proposed using the money to buy the stock or distressed assets of banks and other financial institutions, thereby putting them in a better position to make loans. The government would resell the assets and stock after market conditions improved.

The total amount legislated by Congress in 2008 to address the financial turmoil topped $1 trillion. In February 2009 Congress passed an $800 billion package to stimulate the economy. It was the largest single spending bill in history. In addition to these amounts approved by lawmakers, the Federal Reserve, the FDIC, and the Treasury Department loaned or spent $3 trillion and pledged $6 trillion more if needed to confront the crisis. This sweeping government action increased the national debt significantly.

BARACK OBAMA, HEALTH CARE,
and BIN LADEN

In the midst of the economic downturn, America reached two milestones in the presidential campaign of 2008. Illinois Senator Barack Obama, a Democrat, became the first African-American to win the presidential nomination of a major political party. Even more notable was his election as the 44th president of the United States.

In 2010 President Obama achieved his chief policy goal when he signed a comprehensive health care and insurance reform bill into law. Implemented in stages, the legislation is projected to cost more than a trillion dollars. It calls for increases in taxes, spending, and government regulation while cutting expenditures in some existing programs. A key provision of the law mandates that all citizens obtain health insurance or be subject to penalties. Enforcement is by the IRS.

Technological advances in the oil and natural gas industries led to a boom in exploration and production starting around 2009. Crude oil output surged in Texas* and North Dakota. Natural gas production increased ten-fold in Pennsylvania and more than doubled in Louisiana. In 2014 the U.S. led the world in petroleum and natural gas production and ranked second only to China in coal production.

After a 10-year manhunt, American intelligence agencies located the hiding place of Osama bin Laden in Pakistan. In 2011 President Obama authorized an elite Navy commando unit to storm the compound. Bin Laden was killed in the raid. His body was flown to a U.S. aircraft carrier and buried at sea.

The U.S. pulled all of its forces out of Iraq later that year, bringing the military mission there to a close. Forty-five hundred American troops were killed in the war, and more than 32,000 were wounded.

In 2014 the United States ended combat operations in Afghanistan, although a residual force will remain, mostly in an advisory and training role. The 13-year war claimed the lives of more than 2,300 members of the U.S. military; 20,000 were wounded.

Later in his second term, Obama took executive action to grant legal status and work visas to millions of people living in the U.S. illegally. He also restored diplomatic relations with Cuba and spearheaded negotiations that resulted in Iran agreeing to inspections and limits on its nuclear program in return for the lifting of economic sanctions.

---

* *The modern oil industry began in southeastern Texas in 1901 with the discovery of the Spindletop oil field.*

Americans today face difficult challenges:

- reducing the national debt
- addressing the threats posed by terrorists and aggressive regimes, especially those capable of using weapons of mass destruction
- managing the borders and immigration
- growing the economy, creating jobs, and keeping international businesses competitive
- meeting energy needs
- reducing substance abuse
- educating the rising generation
- being responsible stewards of the environment

History shows that while problems can be daunting, they present opportunities to create a better country and a better world. An understanding of what has gone before gives us a better perspective with which to view current events and anticipate the future. Patrick Henry said, "I know of no way of judging the future but by the past."

Previous generations have passed down to us a stable representative government, a large and productive economy, a beautiful land with natural resources in abundance and rich in variety, and a society with freedoms and a way of life that are the envy of many in the world. Each of us plays a role in determining what our society is now, what kind of world we will leave to future generations, and how our history will be written. Our response to that challenge is one of the ways we show our gratitude for the remarkable legacy we have inherited as citizens of the United States of America.

Selected Bibliography

Ambrose, Stephen E. *Undaunted Courage: Meriwether Lewis, Thomas Jefferson, and the Opening of the American West.* New York: Simon & Schuster, 1996.

Bennett, Lerone. *Before the Mayflower: A History of Black America.* New York: Penguin Books, 1993.

Boyer, Paul S., et al., eds. *The Oxford Companion to United States History.* New York: Oxford University Press, 2001.

Davis, William C. *Look Away! A History of the Confederate States of America.* New York: Simon & Schuster, 2002.

Eltis, David. *The Trans-Atlantic Slave Trade Database.* Emory University. Web. 2016.

Farrand, Max. *The Framing of the Constitution of the United States.* New Haven: Yale University Press, 1976.

Foner, Eric. *Reconstruction: America's Unfinished Revolution, 1863-1877.* New York: Harper & Row, 1988.

Heinrichs, Waldo. *Threshold of War: Franklin D. Roosevelt & American Entry into World War II.* New York: Oxford University Press, 1988.

Keegan, John. *The First World War.* New York: A. Knopf, 1999.

Ketchum, Richard M. *The Winter Soldiers.* Garden City, NY: Doubleday & Co., 1973.

Langguth, A.J. *Patriots: The Men Who Started the American Revolution.* New York: Simon & Schuster, 1988.

Leckie, Robert. *From Sea to Shining Sea: From the War of 1812 to the Mexican War, the Saga of America's Expansion.* New York: Harper Collins, 1993.

Morison, Samuel Eliot, and Henry Steele Commager. *The Growth of the American Republic.* New York: Oxford University Press, 1962.

Morris, Richard B., ed. *Encyclopedia of American History.* New York: Harper & Row, 1965.

Nash, Gary B. *Red, White, and Black: The Peoples of Early America.* Englewood Cliffs, New Jersey: Prentice-Hall, 1982.

Schlesinger, Arthur. *The Almanac of American History.* New York: Putnam, 1983.

Taylor, Alan. *American Colonies*, ed. Eric Foner. New York: Penguin, 2002.

Tindall, George Brown, Charles W. Eagles, and David E. Shi. *America: A Narrative History.* New York: Norton, 1999.

U.S. Bureau of the Census. *Historical Statistics of the United States, Colonial Times to 1957.* Washington, D.C., 1961.

Vaughan, Alden T. *American Genesis: Captain John Smith and the Founding of Virginia.* Boston: Little, Brown and Co., 1975.

INDEX

INDEX

INDEX

INDEX

About the Author

RANDOLPH G. RUSSELL began writing the first and unpublished version of this book for his children, after realizing they did not know many things he assumed they were learning in school. In the course of doing research, he came across numerous surveys showing that the lack of knowledge of basic American history and civics was profound and widespread across all age groups and all academic levels. The book became more sophisticated as a result and has been used at a number of colleges, while remaining easily understood by younger readers.

In addition to his expertise in American history, the author is an accomplished musician who has performed in many European countries and throughout the United States. He holds degrees from the University of Miami and the University of Florida.

61863404R00078

Made in the USA
Charleston, SC
26 September 2016